WORDS OF L♥VE

WORDS OF L♥VE

♥

♥

♥

♥

Penned by
Michael A. Lee

Words of Love
Copyright © 2008 and 2011 by
Michael Andrew Lee

All rights reserved.
No part of this book may be reproduced or transmitted in any form or by any means, electronic, mechanical, including photocopying, recording, or by any information storage and retrieval system, without written permission from the author.

ISBN: 978-0-615-43885-6

Published by: **YAV Publications**
Asheville, North Carolina
YAV books may be purchased in bulk.
For information, please contact Books@yav.com
Visit our website: www.InterestingWriting.com
See last page for author's contact information.

1 3 5 7 9 10 8 6 4 2

Book design by A.M. Lee

Printed in the United States of America
Published February 2011

DEDICATION

To the memory of my loving
and praying grandmother
Mrs. Elizabeth Standback
of Petersburg, Virginia

ACKNOWLEDGEMENTS

No man can do anything by himself and this is what God intends. There are several individuals whose love has helped me complete this book that I wish to acknowledge.

First, to the precious Holy Spirit of God, I give praise and thanksgiving for experiencing what I can best describe as 'divine downloads' from Him. It's as if I have been one of His scribes.

To my beloved wife, Angela, you are a woman of many talents and gifts. You are a walking blessing who keeps giving to all that are around you. Out of your selfless work you found time to encourage me on this quest, (and others). You were the first to believe in its concept and prodded me to press into this work. Your help in the editing and formatting of this my first work in print is invaluable. You are more beautiful than you know, to me and especially to Papa God.

To my parents, Reginald and Margaret Lee. You have raised six children and nurtured them through the many episodes of their lives, including mine. With many prayers and, sometimes, tough love, you have steadily guided me and them: Regina, Annetta, Jerome, David and Noah. You have stayed faithful to God, the church and to each other for more than fifty years. Thank you for being there and not only for us, but for so many others that call you their spiritual mother and father in Christ.

To Mrs. Mable Pierre, my mother-in-law, you are a great example of strength, feistiness, piety and love. I cannot thank you enough for the gifts, which you have given, especially that of your youngest daughter, my wife Angela.

To Bishop Ronald and Phyllis Carter, who through God's grace helped me to see that I could be more. And that God is more than someone you meet on a Sunday morning but also one who is interested in my everyday existence. You loved me, challenged me and mentored me to live a life for Christ. Though many years have passed, the 'Carterisms' have stayed with me. There is no other couple like you in the Body of Christ.

TABLE OF CONTENTS

INTRODUCTION xi

SECTION ONE .... LOVE 1

SECTION TWO .... GOD IS 13

SECTION THREE .... HOME 21

SECTION FOUR .... BLENDING 47

SECTION FIVE .... NATIONS 57

SECTION SIX .... GRACE 75

SECTION SEVEN .... GOD's VARIETY STORE 83

SECTION EIGHT .... LOVE IS 99

INTRODUCTION

GOD IS LOVE. It was out of this unique characteristic that caused Him to send Jesus Christ, His only begotten Son, to live among men, to demonstrate His Kingdom and to die on Calvary so that God the Father could redeem to Himself, the objects of His love...you and I. We are now witnessing a season of gross darkness covering planet earth where swift events are causing many to feel confused, rejected, and unsure of their place; which is influencing multitudes to commit senseless acts of hate, violence and perversion. Yet at the same time, an incredible glory is being revealed from Heaven. The nations are about to know God as He really is. The heavenly Father who cares about every aspect of our lives, desires an increase of His holy family through faith in Jesus Christ and the finished work on the cross.

How did this book come about?

Suddenly, my mind was invaded with these literary expressions of love from Papa God about the object of His affection—the nations of men. As He gave me these words during morning prayer in mid-March of 2008, His envelope of love surrounded me with a pure sweet bliss. I was then impressed to share these words of love, which fill this book in the form of poetry, with those who love the Lord with all their heart and soul. My hope is that those who do not know Him and doubt His existence will begin the trek that ends in their becoming a member of God's holy family. *Words of Love* is also a prophetic work in nature. It is a journey that I believe will be thought provoking, challenging and edifying to you, your family and others around you. It refers to the many issues that are on God's heart and I sought to put them in print as best as I could receive them.

While receiving the poems, one of the lessons I learned and I hope you to discover, is that God loves all people and He speaks to them right where they are. You'll find each section of poems focuses on a certain theme, with each poem leading into its next. Find your favorite and understand that the poem was written with you in mind. I pray that our heavenly Father of love leads you into greater devotion to Him and cause you to see mankind in a different light, through Heaven's eyes. May these words of love and this glimpse into Papa God's heart be a blessing to every reader of this book.

God bless you as you begin the journey into this book

WORDS OF LOVE

SECTION ONE

LOVE

WHO GOD LOVES

I love to bless things
I love to bless you
I love to grow this and you
I love to change things
I love to turn things for you
I love your church
I love your house
I love you more and more

I love to heal
I love to bring your house into change
I love to finance your house
I love to stir you into blessing
I love to hear your prayers
I love to do for you
I love to tell you about my grace
Love hears you
I hear you, love you

Love is doubling in the house
Love brings you into my grace
Love is great, love is abundant
I love doing for this who is in me

Love is a deep thing
Deep it is
Deep it is
A deep well of blessing
It abides, it increases
I love this, I love that
I love this, I love that
They say it's amazing

Watch love blaze in this house
Receive the love that I have
Love will open you to me
Love keeps coming, it keeps coming
Oh love keeps coming
It will cut into this
It will cut and cut this and that
It cuts, but it heals, for it is love

Love for you
Love for you
I do have for you
Love keeps you
Love commands you
Love commands you to purpose
Love hears prayer
Love leads into blessing
Love is a word

It's me!
I love to meet you
I love to lead
I will rest in the church in love

There's love, love, love this day
You're to receive
Receive this day
I love to bring you into my blessing
I love this nation
This nation is great
This nation will turn
Love is blessing the nations

I LOVE YOU MAN

I love you, man
I love your heart
Yes, I love your love
Yes! I love you man
Yes, I love you and your place

Oh I love your house
Rest, rest in me man!
God is love, yes he is
Man, God is abundant
He is here

He is here, you are going to see
Master is showing
The Master is showing
Yeah, God is love
And God loves you man

God is open, he is open for you
He is open today; he is open for you
Papa I AM, papa I AM
Amazed I AM, amazed I AM
Here you see I AM

Grow, open
Grow, open
Man you're to be
You're to be my purpose
Words of blessing

Oh man, where is it?
Oh man, who is this?
Man, where is thee?
Yes, where is thee?
There? Where?

There? Who?
Where? How?
Where? How?
Dad is coming
Here it is

Here it is you're to say
Here it is you're to be
Rest and receive, rest and come in
Love says God is come
Here he is

Watch this day, oh it's day
Amazing love, oh love for you
Man, you're to be
You're to be the one
You're to be in grace

Man
God is coming
You are to be
You are to know
You are to have

Oh God time
God time
God is love and
God loves thee, man!

LOVING

It's loving, it's loving that turns it
They say, is God in this?
I say I do, I do, I do
I say love I do

God loves them
God loves them
He loves them
I Love him, I love him

I love him and I love them
I love him
I love the one
I love the nations

Love abides now
Love abides in this house
It abides in the church
It abides in the house, and oh yes!

It abides in the blessing
It abides in your change
In your change it comes
It opens you to things

Love opens you to things
Love opens the purpose
Love opens—you're blessed!
And you're blessed

And you're blessed
And you're blessed
And you're blessed
And you're blessed

Open, open, open, open
For I come and I come
To turn, to turn, to turn
To turn, to turn, to turn, and to turn

Things will turn, it will turn
I turn your place
I turn your house
I turn for I do; I turn for I do

I turn for I do; I turn for I do
I do, I do, I do
I do, I do, I do for you
Yes, I do for you

IT'S LOVE YOU ARE

Love
It's love you are
It's love you are
It's love you are
It's love you are for them to me
Oh love these
And love receive

BROAD, BROAD, BROAD

It's broad, broad, broad
It is broad but it is open
It is open in grace
It is open in blessing
It is open in love
It is open to me!
It is open to go
It is open to abide
It is open to receive

THE BLESSING IS IN YOU

Oh the blessing is in and in and in
Oh the blessing is in you
Oh you are the blessing

Blessing opens things
The blessing's coming
But it's now on you

The blessing is on your church
The blessing is on your seed
The blessing is in your house

Oh the blessing is in your church
The blessing is on you
The blessing is sharing

The blessing is on you…rise
The blessing is on you…arise
The blessing is showing

It's showing and showing
The blessing is seeding
The blessing is sowing and sowing

The blessings are commanding
The blessings are commanding
You to receive

Sight, sight, sight
It's sight for you
The blessing you're to receive

LOVE BLESSING

It's time to be a blessing
But it's time to have and receive
You are loved, you are loved
This blessing is to say
You are loved, loved, loved

Blessing on your place
Blessing on your place
Blessing on your house
Blessing on your love
Blessing on your house

Blessing on your place
Blessing on you
Yes, blessing on you
Blessing on your blessing
Blessing in you

Blessing here and there
Oh blessing you are

God is daddy, God is daddy
Yes blessing, blessing, blessing
Amazing blessing, amazing love
Amazing, you are now loved
Yes blessed and blessed

You are blessed
Blessed in things
Blessed in dreams
And blessed in visitation
God blesses: you are blessed

Oh the door opens for you
Oh blessed you are
Dad loves blessing
The word is the blessing
And you are to receive

Love connects and love connects
Love connects and love opens

Rise, receive
Rise and see
Blessing in things
And rise and do
And rise and leap

Oh it's blessing
God is blessing
Receive!
Raising, going
Raising and going

It's blessing grace
It's blessing words
It's blessing now
It's blessing show
God does and God loves

It's now blending
It's now bringing

Diverse, diverse
Diverse things
Love blessing, love blessing
Grace opens things
God loves growing and blessing

Doors open and doors hear
Your door opens
And your doors answer
God opens heaven
He opens for you

He opens for you

THE DEBT

The debt, the debt, love turns this
The debt is me I turn, for I turn
Love turns this, debt is turned
Love is turned to blessing
Love is turned to finance

It's turned to visit
It's turned to a blowing
And now love turns it
It turns what was
What was into abundance

Abundant love
Abundant grace
It's growing into abundance
Love will blow blessing
It blows utter blessing

Love leads into blessing
I love to bless and blow blessing
Love leads in blowing in
For it's love, love, love
It's love in me, it's love receive

Love, love, opens the blessing
Love, love, opens a house
Love increases abundance
Yea, love will turn a thing
Love will turn a thing into a blessing

Yes
Oh yes
Oh yes
You will see
Love lane

LOVE-A-ME

It's join! Join! Join!
It's a joining! It's a joining!
What they say, a joining!
It's joining man and man
It's joining nation and nation

They say the light is in this
But my words are light
They are light
My words are light

They are grace
They are blessing
They are dreams
They are visitations
They are grace

These are hours to be
These are hours to me
These are hours of love
These are hours of healing

These are hours of dreams
These are grand days
These are days of new love
These are days to new blessing
These are days to bring blessing

These are days
To love me
These are
Days to
Love
Me

WHERE IS LOVE??

They say it's in Buddha
And they say it's in 'a one'
They say you're to see who this is
But love is in me and love is in me

They say love is in a 'ut'
And love is in a top
And love is in a can
They say love is in a tumble
They say love is in a tumble
They say love is in a 'ho'

They say love is in a 'ut'
And they say love is in a thing
And they say love is in a thing
And in a thing, is a thing

They say love is in a thing
They say love is in a—what??
They say love is in the thing
They say love is in this

And love is in that
They say love is in—oh that!
They say love is in
Who that is
Love they say
Love is in bun, bun, bun

They say love is in a part
They say love is in this part, that part
They say love is in a shoe
They say love is an up and up

They say oh, oh, oh this I love
They say love, oh that?
They say love what?
They say love is uh and uh
They say love is uh-huh
They say this? That? This?

I say love is me
They say love is in London
They say love is in Paris
They say love is in tumble & tumble

I say love is in me
I say love is in me
Gender, gender
Gender, gender
They say love is in a gender
Love says it's in me

And love is now in me

I AM LOVING

The love you receive
Is a love of my grace
The love you receive
   Is a love of me
The love you have
   Is me for you
And Yes! Yes! Yes!
It's love you receive
   For I AM

LOVE STAYS

Love stays
It stays in my grace
It stays in my abundance
It stays in my love
It stays in my abundance
It stays, it stays
It stays in me

Oh it does increase in you
Oh it does increase in that
Oh it does increase in days
Oh it does open days

It's a stay, it's a stay
It's a stay, it's a stay
Oh it's a stay today
Oh it's a great utter thing

Oh God stays
He stays in purpose
Oh love is a stay
You're to stir love

GENERATION LOVE: IT IS NOT LATE

They say this is not this
This is not this
Late, late, they say
This is now late
But I say now is day
Love is in this nation
Love is in this church

SOME LOVE WORDS

They say roger and roger
I say open and go
They say roger, roger
But I say you're to go and go

You're to go in nations
You're to go in places
You're to go in abundance
You're to go in blessing

It's the key to purpose
It's the key to open door
It's the key to love
For it is the key in

For it is the open thing
It's the open door
What a door you go in!
It's the open door

You go and go and go
What a door, what a door
What a door!
Oh, oh what a door!
I will turn the door

God says go in the door
I send you: go in
Love says it is what you see
You go, and as you go, you see

BLESSING GENERATION

This is a blessing generation
Love loves them

There's a gust
And the gust is the gust of love
Love is a gust
It's a gust of purpose

Love blesses them
Love blesses this house
My love is a great love
My love is a blessing love

My love hears
The words of your house

Love is a love that loves

AN OMEN FOR THE CHURCH

Love is a word they say
Love is a purpose this day, I say
God, God, God time!
It's God's time for love
For now it's my time

Love in the church
Love in your house
Love in my house
Love in my honor
And love in grace
And love in grace

IT'S TO LOVE

It's to love, it's to love
It's to love, it's to love
It's to love mercy, it's to love honor
It's to love them, it's to love these
It's to love them who are in this
It's to love; love will lead
This is love
It's me

LOVE PREAMBLE

Love the one
Love the one
You're to love the one
Yes, love to them
Yes, I tell you to say
And say love in this

I send you in, in-love
I send you in to love
I send you in my blessings
I send you in my blessings
And I send you, and I send you
And I send you…and I send

WORDS OF LOVE

SECTION TWO

GOD IS

AMAZING

It's amazing, I AM
It's amazing, I receive
It's amazing what I AM
It's amazing what I AM

It's amazing you are loved
It's amazing you are loved
It's amazing that you are
Loved and loved
I am amazing and I am abundant

Amazing, love's grace
Amazing, love's abundance
Oh I am love, I am love
It's love, love, love

Love, oh what love
Oh what love for thee!
Love is mighty, but it is amazing
Oh it's amazing, but it's my love

Deed, love is a deed
Dad is in the deed
A deed for abundance
A deed for love

It's a deed for showers of grace
It's a deed for love's blessing
Amazing, oh amazed
Oh amazing…what it is
Rhyme, rhyme, rhyme, rhyme

Amazing, amazing
It's amazing
Abundant, and abundant
But it's amazing, for it's abundant

Last, last, for blessings come
For blessings come for this church
Love, amazing love
Maker, maker, love is amazing

Love abundant; love amazing
Love is a hope and love is amazing

THE FORCE

The force...what is it?
The force is the word
The force is the word of blessing
The force is a change in things
The force is changing churches

The force is blessing you
The force is blowing and going
The force is the power of grace
The force...oh what is it?
The force is a time of blessing

The force is a visit
The force is a grace

But the force is papa
The force is blessing
The force is blending
The force is visiting
The force is wide and the force is wide

The force is open, oh yes!
But the force, where is it?
But the force, the force...is me!
The force is showing
The force is sowing

The force is my grace
The force is changing your church

The force, the force, the force, yes!
The force is my grace
The force is love
The force is great blessing
And it's my love

But the force is more and more
The force is blessing
The force is lifting and lifting
But the force is doing and going
The force is showers of open heavens

But the force is resting in your house
The force is more open, you're seeing

But the force is more and more
The force is blessing
The force is lifting and lifting
But the force is doing and going
The force is showers of open heavens

But the force is resting in your house
The force is more open, you're seeing
The force is daddy, daddy
Eden, Eden, Eden
God is going to receive blessing

The blessing is here
The blessing is the force

The blessing is the force
And the force is here
The blessing's working in your house
The blessing's going to teach & teach
The force increases and blesses

The force: blustery wind
The force is daddy working
But the force is daddy's words
The force is papa and blessing
The force is wide and great

The force is daddy, waking and going
The force, there's the force

The force is going into your house
The force is dad, dad, dad!
And the force is sons and dad
The force is blowing in change
The force is doing in your church

But the force is lifting and lifting
The force is bold yes! God is the force
The force is 'mazing
The force is open
The force is working

Love is going to show
Love is here...love is a force

The Force - (continued)

It's your love that turns things
Your love is turning your change
The force is power
The force is leaping up and going
The force is doing in thee

Oh what is this thing?
What is this thing?
God is the force
It's going, it's being: God is in this
Daddy's wide and daddy's great

And he is the great one
He is the great, great, blessing

There's a great door that is healing
This is the time for this purpose
The force...yes it is the day
The force, oh God is the force
The force blends and the force keeps

The force is in days
And in times and in seasons
The force is the great changing
The force is the answer to this and this
This day is the day of the force

The nights are coming
The nights are coming

The nights are the knights of the force
The force is going to turn a house
The force will turn a nation
Each door is a door for me

LIGHT

Light, light, light
There's a light here, there's a light here
Light here, light now
The light is the word

My word is light
It's the words of grace
There's a gem: this is the word
This is light: I-AM-THAT-I-AM

I send love, I send light
I send love, I send great light
You are in me. Yea!
You are in me!

It's a depth
My love is light
Oh it's a deep word
It's a deep grace

Oh what grace!
Oh great light!
Oh great light, great light!
Oh love's light!

Yes, my love is the great light
The light, the light
The word is the light
Oh! What light it is!

SHOWERS

God is in the showers
He is in the rain
He is in a great shower
Oh he is in the rain
Watch this great rain
A rain of works, a rain of grace
Love opening the heavens
Love is a great shake
Oh but it's a great abundance of rain

WORDS OF LOVE

SECTION THREE

HOME

BLESSED HOME

The house, the house
Dine, dine in the house
Oh the house, open now
The house is great in my purpose

Oh this house is a word house
This house is an open grace
This house is a love place. They ask
Oh how is this a place for me?

Oh me, it's me
The blessing is in the house
The love is in this place
The love is for the nation

The love is dad and his seed
Oh he loves, he loves, he loves
He loves his house
He loves his church

Oh he loves to bless
Oh he loves to come
He loves to change
He loves to see

Binding grace, binding grace
It's the place, the place for me
The place to be—oh yes today
Oh yes! Ah-ha, ha-ha

Oh blessing the house
The house, the house
The house is abundant
Oh abundance of me

Oh love is there
Oh love is here
The love opens nations
The love opens a church

Oh I tell them
Oh there's great love
Oh love for man, love for the man
Race, race, race for blessing

Love says, love here
There's love there and love this
Love is a voice in this house
Love is a great house

And love is a place to be
Love is in this place
My love hears
The words of your house

Love is a love that loves

FATHERS, FATHERS, FATHERS

Fathers, fathers, fathers
Fathers hear my love and do
Is love in thee? Is love in thee?
Grow and be the fathers to them

Be and be the fathers to them
Stir the love and stir the blessing
Stir the love and stir the abundance
Stir the blessing, stir the blessing

Correct, bless, correct
Love them, love them, love them
Do this, be this, love these, love these
The beat of the word
The beat of the word
You're to be, you're to be

THE FATHERS

The body, oh the body
It's the body of grace
The body is a great change
The body is a great shedding

God is blending, blending
God is showing and hearing
God is seeing and seeing
And God is sowing and sowing

It's fathers, fathers
It's fathers for my grace
It's fathers of my abundance
They are fathers of my love

The fathers are coming
The fathers are loving
They are loving and they are coming
God is sending and sending

Oh they are the fathers
Oh they are the fathers
Oh love and love
Oh watch these now

Watch! They are open
Oh they are the fathers
Oh love and love opens them to me
Days of blessing and days of blessings

Arise, father, arise
Watch the fathers open
The fathers of grace and
The fathers of abundance

Oh the fathers, oh the fathers
Oh great is this time
Love is in this and this
Oh things are going to be

Dad, dad, dad
It's time to be, it's time to see
Walk and walk and walk
It's time to come and time to show

There's a daughter and there's a seed
But there's a son, there's a seed
Oh it's time to be, it's time to love
Oh dad, oh father, it's time

WHO IS DADDY?

Who is daddy? It's me!
It's amazing what I am
Daddy, who is he?
It's who I AM

There's a bar seat
Daddy, who is he?
Who is he they say
Oh I AM, but I AM

Amazing what they say
Amazing about my grace
Deciding, deciding
Where, who and how

Dad, they say who? Where?
They say where is he
Dad I AM. Dad I see
Dad loves, dad loves

Dad loves to be
Oh I love, and I love, and I love
I love these, I love who
I love these, I love you

Motive? It's me
Daddy? Where?
It's me you see
Daddy loves to show he IS

Daddy rots; they say daddy rots
They say he rots and rots
Bad old, bad old
They say he's an odd one

Love is dad; love is blessed
There's a peace: I AM open to you
You are loved, you are loved
I AM love, I AM love

DAD'S STANDING

The office, the office
The office is changing
The office is blowing
The office is changing

The office: where is he?
He, where is dad?
Where is dad? Who is he?
Love is he, love is me

Love is blowing in the office
And love is blowing in the blessing
Love is blending, love is growing
Love is blending, love is me

Love is blending, love is me
Love is leaping into these
Love is dad who is here
He is now in the place

Why, they say; where, they say
What is this? And where is he?
Where is the one?
Where is dad?

The matter is in being
It's the matter of doing
It's me to be
It's blending, it's blessing

Love, God says love
It's time to be
Love says dad
Come dad…now you're to be

DAD DOES

Dad is abundant
Dad is abundant
Oh he does bless
He is abundant to do for you
Happily
He is in grace

God is open: I am open
Destiny dad
Oh destiny he
God is dad and dad is he
Dad here, dad here
God is dad, and God is dad

DAD LOVES TO BE

Dad loves to be
He loves to show
Oh dad loves to rest
Oh he loves to shed

He loves to shed love
He loves to shed grace
He loves to shed grace
And loves to grow and grow

Oh love is one who's me
He is a loving dad
He is a great dad
God loves, he loves

He loves growing and being
He loves being and doing
He loves great and least

God is blowing, God is loving
He is bringing, he is showing
God is leaping, God is leaping
He is being, he is blending

Oh raising, oh loving
Oh bringing, oh going
He is leading, he is working
He is going, he is going

Oh, oh he is loving
He is working, but he is doing
There's a working and working
Here, love is in dad

Love is in dad

HE'S HOME! DADDY'S HOME!

Oh you see?
Oh you see?

He is now in the house
He is now in the house
He is now in this place

He is now in the house
He is now blessing
He is now going...doing
He is now here

He is dad
He is dad
He is dad

He is now in the house
Here, here, here, here!
He is now in my house!

DAD AND DAUGHTER

Dad and daughter
God is in dad and daughter
God is dad and God is dad
He is dad, oh he is great

He is love, he loves daughter
He loves to bless his daughter
He loves to bless his seed
He loves daughter, he loves now

DAUGHTER RICH

God is abundant
Blessing in grace
Daughter loves—daughter has
Yes, daughter hears the blessings

Love great, love hears
Love shows, love blesses
Love hops, love hears
Love operates blessings

Labor, love hears
Lace, lace, lace
Love blesses, blesses, blesses
Love blesses, love operates

Diamond, diamond
Diamond, diamonds
Love is a great blessing
Love hears and abundance hears

It's a love hearing—love showing
Love hears and love blesses
Love great and great abundance
A daughter loves, a daughter sees

Love is a great sharing
Love, abundant love
Love loves blessing
The daughter is abundant

Love is a satin in grace
Rich, rich! Yes, you're seeing
Love blesses, blesses and blesses
Love shows abundance

And love blesses and love increases
God's ready, ready he is
God's blessing
Abundance, abundance

Love grace, love here
God is abundant and abundant yes
Greater grace—greater operation
Many blessings—open grace

Ready now, ready now

THE DAUGHTER, THE DAUGHTER

The daughter, oh I receive
Oh I receive this who is in me
Oh this daughter is loved
Oh this daughter is me

The daughter, oh I receive
The daughter, oh she is loved
Oh this daughter is here
Oh this one is abundant

Daddy is abundant, daddy is abundant
Daughter, oh you are open to blessing
Daughter, you are blessed and loved

Oh daughter I love
Daughter, hear it!
Daughter, receive it!
Daughter you are in me
Daughter you are in me

Daughter, oh yes, receive
Daughter you are open to receive
It's said that you're old
And you're not...you are in me
You are abundant—receive!

It's abundant love, it's abundant love
Settle not! Settle not!
Increase, increase, increase
Dad answers, dad answers

Daddy does, daddy does
Dad abundant, dad of grace
Daddy does, daddy abides
Oh he is blessing, he is blessing

Yes, he is love
God is abundant
Oh I receive daughter
Oh daughters, oh I love

THE DAUGHTERS ARE OPEN

The daughters are open to grace
The daughters are open to love
The daughters are open to love
The daughters are abundant and loved

Daughters, daughters, daughters
Oh daughters, loved and loved
Daughters, loved you are
Oh daughter, love receive

Wider, wider is my grace
Oh it's a wide love I send
It's a wide love I send
It's a wide love I tell

It's dad doing, dad receiving
Sadie, God is abundant
Matter you do! Matter you do!
It's me you are in

Oh the love you receive
Body, body, body, open yourself in grace
God is open, God is open
Oh the body is abundant

Daughter, daughter
Daughter loved, daughter loved
Daughter, love you!
You are open, you are in me

DADDY'S DAUGHTERS

Daddy's daughters, daddy's daughters
Love, love, I love
Love I have for the daughters
Love for the daughters
The love for the daughters
I love the ladies
Love loves the ladies
Loving, loving, loving these
Love is a word for the daughters
Daddy, daddy, daddy sees
Ready blessed the daughters are
The daughters, oh the daughters
The letters, the letters, the letters
The letters God sends
Dad is a dad of grace
There are many men, many things
Many shut this
Dead, dead, they say it's dead
Date and date
They say date this, date that
They say things, but they say things
Daughter, daughter, daughter I say
I am your answer
I am your one
Road abundant, it's road abundant
Maiden, maiden
Oh maiden—I AM
Rest in love
Rest in love
A man you receive is a man in love
God says he loves blessing
He loves grace
He loves change
He loves me
Men there are
Men there are
Adding, they come
Rest in me, and rest in my grace

THE BLADE—THE WORD

The blade—the word
The word is the key
The word is to change
The word is to abide

This is the day of operation: shatter
Set days these are
These are days of honors, honors
The body is abundant

This is the day
For the mantle to come
This is the day for blessing now
For God is abundant

Dad loves me
Dad loves thee
Daughters and sons
Ways of grace

Blessings on the sons and daughters
Start to receive the daughters
And start to have sons
The watch is a generation

Daughters and sons now come
Daughters and sons are now to come

Daddy, daddy, daddy abides
Blessing, blessing, blessing open things
The blessing is now
And the blessing is abundant

The blessing is now
The blessing is now
Oh the blessing now is
Sally, Sally, now I bless

Dad, dad, dad loves
Oh I love to send the secrets
These are love-sharings
Dad, dad operates

Daughter, son, love yes
Maker loves, he loves
Oh daddy, daddy loves thee
Bright, bright, bright is this sharing

Bright is this word
Love, love, love them
Love, I love to show you
Love, I love to abide now

Love I show and I show
It's love here, love now
Love odd…love yeah
Love me? Love yes!

Love yes, love grow
Love, love, love this
Love more—love this
Shake the rod, shake the rod

The rod of blessing, the rod of grace
The rod of God—the rod is now

It's dad, it's dad
Dad, dad, dad operates
Love is a day for this day
Dad's day is now

And dad's day is here
Oh love operates for this now
Love blending, love operating
The matter is grace

The Blade—The Word: (continued)

The matter is operating
The matter is changing

Oh fathers, fathers
Oh fathers you are
The finance you receive
To bless your seed

Daughters, sons, receive
They receive—you receive
They receive light and blessing
Daughters, sons, now abide

There's a shower
It's a shower of blessings
Lads, lads, lads, lads
Rising, rising, rising, the lads

They say dad he is not
But I say he is, yes he's here, he's here
Rebels? But they're seers
Daughters and sons

Letters come, letters come
Letters now, letters now

Date, date, date, date
Oh the date is now, worship
Daughter—dad, daughter—dad
It's dad and daughter

Matter, matter, matter, matter
The days matter
Lad, lad, lad, lad
But it's me: dad, dad, dad

Oh my seed, oh my seed
Blending, blending
God is blending
Rising love, it's rising

Oh love rising

DAD IS LOVE

Dad is love
Dad is love: oh how he sees
Dad is love: blessing and doing
God is dad, God is dad

Dad ways are my grace
Dad is way blessed
Dad is way abundant
Oh, oh dad is great!

Dad is way great
And dad is way out
Way out, way oh!
Way in, way out!

Dad, oh dad; oh he is abundant
Daughters, daughters, daughters
They are blessed
Sons yes, sons, blessed, blessed

Daughters, sons
Dad, dad, oh he is abundant
Make it, make it…you will make it!
D-days, D-days…it's Dad Days

Oh I will see the ones
Dad is open, dad is open
Broke, broke, broke
But abundant you are

The word blessed is blessed
The blessor is he, the blessor is he
God is blessing
God is dad and God is dad

Dad is way, he is way blessed
He's way abundant
He's way abundant
He's way love

Said, said, said
They say God is old and God is old
It's opposite: it's love, it's love he is!
It's a seed in me

Oh the love of the dad
It's dad open in me
Dad is abundant
He is abundant

Grow it. Be it
Rejoice for me in thee
Better, better, better now
Daughter, daughter, daughter, I bless

Son yes! Son, I see and I see
Daughter, daughter
Watch my words
And secrets, secrets, secrets you have

Amazing
Amazing I AM
God is love, God is dad
God is love and God is dad

SONS-DAUGHTERS-SONS

Sons blessed, sons loved
Sons are my sons
The sons are loved
The sons are loved

The daughters are loved
Daughters of grace
It's daughters of love
Yes, the daughters, they are loved

It's a word, it's a blessing
And sons, and sons, and sons
The sons are my sons
Sons who are my sons

Daughters are blessed
Daughters are blessed
Daughters are loved in my grace

Market, market, market
It's in the markets you are in
The markets of grace
The markets of abundance

Oh my secrets
Oh my secrets
Oh my secrets
Oh my secrets

Oh the sons, oh the sons
Oh they are open to me
They are more in the grace
And they are more in my purpose

Double lies, double lies
They say daddy is upset
Daddy is uptight
Dad is shut, dad is shut

But dad is not this
Dad is blessing
Dad is love and
Dad is love

Oh I AM abundant
It's a broad word
It's a broad time
It's dad's love for these

Discern, discern my grace
I am going to tell you
Love in sons
Love in daughters

DADDY BLEND

Oh it's daddy blend
It's daddy and daddy and daddy
It's daddy and the seed
Oh daddy is in the seed
Oh daddy is in the seed

Oh daddy is blending grace and love
God is a dad of grace
Oh God is a dad of great love
Yes, dad is a blending
Oh dad blending love and grace

It's dad and seed
Yes, dad and son
Yes, God is dad and they are seed
Blazing a great grace
Blazing a great grace

God blending grace
Blustery love
God is blending
Blending and blending
Love, oh, ah-ha!
Ha-ha!

LOVE IS A 'POP'

Love is a pop: a pop of blessing
Love is a pop: a pop of blessing
Love is who blesses
For love is man who is blessed

It's a love that blessed
It's a love of the one
A love of one who is the one
A love of one who is the one

The one who is the one
One is the pop who says
Yes, yes, yes, yes, yes!
Oh yes you are: you are my blessed!

Who is the one who says you're blessed?
He is who says he is
Oh he is pop
And pop says words

He says: love
He says: blessing
He says: I AM
He says: you are
Love says: blessed!

He says you are mine and you are mine
He says I AM
He says see me! I AM
He says love I send
And he says blessed, blessed, blessed I see

Love says oh blessed
He says blessed and blessed
He says love is me
He says love blesses
He says love is words: words of blessing

Love is the words I say of blessing
I say blessing
For love and love and love
For it's my purpose
Love is me

And love is POP!

LOVE IS A DAD

Love is a dad who opens his grace
Love is a dad who blesses his house
Love is a word that blesses a church
Love is an amazing dream

I am open to you
But I am open to you and they
The battle for your nation
Watch these days
For your mantle is abundant
Destined to bring, destined to bring
Destined to abide in this nation
Dad, who is dad?
I am the one you are to come to
Dad I am, dad I am
God says dad I am

Love to them
Love is a word, but I AM
This is a seed for me to be
They are mine…I am in them

DADDY-GOD

Daddy-God, it's daddy-God
Money, money I send
God says I send love
Blessing, blessing, blessing

Love-blessing
Love-abundance
Love-shed
Love-grace

God says love-grace
Ride in me, ride in me
Ride in me, ride in grace
Ride in abundance

Rain, rain
Raining abundance
Daddy-bless
Yes, daddy-bless!

IT'S DAD'S DAY

Master, master grace
Love is the key to my grace
Oh, oh yes! Dad is now
Arms of grace and arms of grace

Dad is loving, dad is loving
He is love, he is love
He is abundant, he is here
Master of grace, master of grace

Love is dad's thing
And love is my blessing
Love is my power
And love is blessing and grace

Love is a mantle for my house
Love is a power to change
But love is more of my power
And love is here, oh yes it is

Rise! Rise!
Here I am! Here I am!
Oh my secret, my love is great
Amazing what I do
Amazing what I do

Oh God is here, God is now
Here he is, here he is
More love is more here
Ready, ready, yes here it is

Dad you're destined to receive
Dad you're destined to know
Reach and receive; reach and receive
Here, oh here is he

Labor…but receive
Oh receive my command
Oh receive my command
God-dad, God-dad

The Master is sharing
He is sharing
Love comes as you receive
Rest in me…love is a here

Love is a change
Oh God is in this house
Oh love is a time to be
But love is opening up and up, oh up

Blend, oh blend
God is doing
God is doing, oh he's doing
Master loves
The Master loves

DADDY'S CHANGING THINGS

Daddy's changing things
Daddy's going in
Daddy's doing now
Oh daddy loves to change

Oh he comes, he comes

He comes to turn
He comes to turn
He comes to turn
He comes to bless

IT'S DADDY'S WAY

It's daddy's way: open heavens
Blessing: dad blesses, dad hears
Dad heeds and dad loves
Dad heeds: wider, wider, wider

Dad loves, dad loves
Dad loves, oh he does, he does
It's dad's, dad's, dad's thing
Oh it's dad's things

Oh dad is way blessing
Oh dad is way here
Oh he is way more
He is way out!

Oh dad's way, oh dad's way

DADDY LOVES

Ready, ready, ready
Daughters, sons, daughters
Dad, dad, dad, oh dad here
Dad, son; dad, daughter

Raising, raising, raising these
God is love, and love is this
God is love and love is this
Mighty grace, mighty love

Teaching grace, teaching love
Daddy loves this house
Daddy loves this seed
Great love, great love

Ready, receive; ready, see
Rising love, rising blessings
Love shows, love rests
Oh blessing love: blessing these

LOVE DAD

Love dad
Love dad
Love dad

I love to be
I love to do
I love to send

But I love, I love and I love
God is great, God is love
Love is me
I receive your blessings
I receive your word
It's me, it's me
Oh love in thee
Daddy, daddy, daddy is me
Blessing, blessing, blessing, yes!

Dad is love
Dad is love
The love I see

Oh it's love blessing
Dad oh
Dad is love

THE HOBBLE

The hobble is a turn
A turn to blessing
This is a turn to blessing
For it is a turn to purpose

This is a turn to growing
This is a turn to love
This is a turn to purpose
And it is a turn to me

They say it's an arid place
It's a place for the purpose
It's a place of growing
It's a place of seeing
It's a place of abiding
It's a place of love
It's a place who I am

They say oh this is old now
They say it's an old place
But I say it's in this
In this there is purpose
It's in purpose to abide

They say oh, oh where?
They say where, they say where?
I say know it's in this
It's in this there's purpose
It's purpose to turn

It's purpose to turn
It's purpose is to cut
It's purpose is to cut that and that
It's purpose is to cut what they say

They say this, they say that
But I say this is you
You are a great one: a son, a son
You are one: a one whose mine

You are one who is a one
You are one who is a one
A one of word
A one of blessing
A one of healing
A one of abundance
A one of abiding

A one of answers
It's you, it's you, it's you. Yes!
It's you! It's you that is a one
This is what you're to see
This is you

Love is the one that turns
The one who turns the words
The one who hears them
Love is a purpose
They will see

The Hobble - (continued)

What they say...they say
Love says you are: you see, you see?
You see, you see, you see? You see?
Do you see that you are in me?
I AM the one: you are in me

And yes, you are a one
You are a one in my grace
You are a one in my house
God is love, and he loves to turn it
He is love, he loves to bless

You are loved
You are blessed
You are a son
A son of blessing, a son of word
It's a word of blessing
Love, love hears things
Love hears things: who says that

Love hears their word
And he says, you are a one
A one of blessing
A one of answers
A one of abundance
Love says you are in me
You are in me: a son

THE GENERATIONS

Watch these days
Watch what you see
There is a God, there is a God
There is a God
There is a great, great God

Months these be
These are months of abundant power
These are months of great power
These are months of open heavens

And months and months
And months and months!

Months of open doors
Months of leaders, leaders, leaders
Months of operations
Months of commands

These are days of blessings
And days of great grace
And days where you know
Who I AM
And watch me in *this!*

Blood, but blessing
And abundance of finances
And abundance of love
And abundance of grace

Blessings open up on the generations
And blessings will turn this generation

Barren, but blessed
Barren, but abundant
Barren but open
And barren but healed
And barren but opened

And blessing and blessing and blessing
And works and works and works
And worship, worship, worship
And open heaven
Open heaven, open heaven

Watch, watch, watch!
Watch! The mantle falls on them
They are the seed
And they are the sons

And they are the seed
And they are the seed

And they are open to me
Love opens them to me
They are what you know
They are who you see

They are your seed
Who are they?
They are the seed
They are the sons
And they are your sons

My blessing—my blessing
Oh they are a great blessing
Oh they are my power
And they are my purpose

And they are now in the purpose
And they are most in this and that

They are—oh!
What they in?
My son, they are in purpose
But they are in this and that
And now I send them to this

Generations - (continued)

I send them to the church
They are blessed, they are blessed
They are blessed, they are blessed
They are loved, they are word

God blesses this
They are open to me
Oh you're to have and receive!
They are in me

Why they do this?
Why they go there?
Why they be this?
Why they show this?

They are in me
They are open to me
They are abundant in me
And they are now to be

Blessed and blessed!
Oh motors
Motor, motor, motor
There's a new growing

Labor, they labor
They labor on my blessing
They blend with your church
They're a bridge to the nations

They are abundant in your church
You're to have, you're to have
You're to have
They come, they come

They come!
Oh the word for them is
It's love
Love, love

LOVE IS A BOY AND HIS DAD

It's a boy, it's dad
It's a dad, it's his seed
Things and things are in grace
God is dad, God is dad

Ready, ready
God is blessing
God is blessing the son
God is blessing the son
God is hearing the son
God is healing and God is healing
God is healing the son

He's healing, he's dressing
He's here, he's here!
He's here and now!
He's here to see
He's here to hold
He's here to love
He's here to blend
He's here to show
He's here to change

It's now leaping, it's now loving
It's now grace, it's now leaping

Blend, blend, the blending
Love is the son and the dad
God says blending, God says blending
It's a great love blending
It's love, it's me
It's here, it's here

Oh love is a son and it's a dad
It's a son who is in grace
It's a son in grace
It's a rich grace
It's a love of blessing
It's a love of the seed

But it's my son
And my son
And my son
It's my son and my seed

WORDS OF LOVE

SECTION FOUR
BLENDING

I'M BLENDING

God says I'm blending
The blend of great
The blend of grace
God is blending

God is blending
It's blending man and grace
Blending more and love
Blending seed and change

It's blending money…blending love
Love and grace, love and grace
Love and grace hears blessings
Blessing more, blessing grace

God blend, God blend
God blend, love blend

My grace
Love blend I do
Love blend, love grace
The manner is blending

The lad, the lady receives blessing
Amazing, abundant grace
Love is a blend of me and thee
Love is an odd thing

It's an odd thing
Oh it's a great thing
Love is a sharing of me and thee
Love is a sharing of me and they

Blending, oh I blend
Love is a blending and I blend
Love is a great leap into me
Blending, blending

And great blending
Lady joy, lady joy
Love blends you and my grace
Love blends a part and a part

God is dancing, he is dancing
He is dancing, he is here
He is dancing, oh he is love
The Master loves, the Master loves

The Master loves
And the Master sows

Oh the Master great
And the Master hears
The Master loves
The Master grows

Dad the Master, dad the Master
Love is a great blend
Love is a blend of more and you
Love is a blend of here and there

But love is of me and thee
God is a-blending
God is a-blending
God is a-blending

LOVE BLEND

Love blend: God is love, God is love
Love is a blend of blessings
It's love blend, love grace
Love is a blend and love is open

Dad blends, dad loves
Love is a great love
Love is a blending of hope
And open heaven

It's a blend of leaders and me
It's a blend of man and
A blend of abundance
Dad is going to preach

Dad is going to love
Love is a blend of hearts
Love is a blend
Who is in this?

Love is the blend
Of the woman and the man
Love is the blend for these
For love is the blend of my grace

For love is the blend
Of time and time
Dad is a-blending
And dad is a-blending

Love is a great blessing for you
Daddy blending: he is
Love is a leap into me
Blending and abundant

Oh blending is love
Love blend

LOVE IS A BLEND

It's the blend, it's love
Love is my blend
Love is a blend
It blends me with this
It blends you and me

Love blends you and blends me
It blends me to your place
It blends you with my blessing
It blends you to receive
It blends my blessings in your heart

Oh I blend you, I blend
You I blend with my blessing
I love to bless and I love to blend
I love to blend you
And blend you in me

Love is a blend
Oh it's a wonder-blend
It's a wonder of words
It's a wonder of blessing
Love, love, love, I do

Love I do
Love is me, love is me
I do bless in you
I do blend you and you

Love blending, I blend you
I blend you in me
I blend you…loving you

Love is a leading, love is a reading
Love is a word, love is my word
Love is my word, my word for you
Love is my word to you…for you

THE BLEND

Yes! Oh blend!
Blend of me and you
Blessing of love and abundance
It's a blessing of love
Oh love is a blend
It's a blend of me and grace
Yes, here and there
Yes, love is a blend of here and there
Yes, my love is a blend
Love is a blending of meat and grace
God is a great love
And God is a great love
Love is a blend of my and you
Love is a blend of here and yes

Dad blending, dad blending
Love is a blending of grace and grace
Love is a blending of man and God

It's a blend of amazing love
Blending of God and love
Yeah, what is this great thing?
Oh great is this blend
It's a blend of me, it's a blend of here
It's a destiny of grace
It's a destiny of a great thing
Love seed, love seed
Rest days, rest days
Love is a great blend
Love is a great blending
Reach, reach for this great thing
Reach for blessing and love
Oh reach for abundance and love

Love is a blend
Oh blend!

LOVE BLENDING

Oh blending, blending, blending
It's love blending
It's blending workings
Oh it's blending grace
Love blending
Oh great abundance

There's love
Oh love, oh love, oh love
But there's blessing
And blessing and blessing
There's grace and grace and grace
But there's my love

THE SIGN IS…

There's a sign, there's a sign
The sign of blessing
The sign is now
Oh it's the sign of blessing
The sign is great, great, connection
The sign is the love-blend
It's the sign of blessings and grace
Love is a sign
Leap up! Grow in!
Leap up! Be it!
The sign
Oh the sign…is thee

LOVE BLEND II

Love is a blending of great change
Love is a blending of words and song
Love is a blending of he and she
But it is a blend of me and thee

SUCH LOVE

Such love, there's such love
I love to blow in
They say it is a start
I say, it's the time
I say it is now
It's time for the purpose
It's time for the healing
It's time for abundance
It's time for blessing love

Love says it's my blowing
Love is in this and that
They say who is an elder?

There is a blowing-and-a-blowing
There is a word-and-a-word
It's a-healing-and-a-healing
It's a healing blessing
They say blend?
Blend??
But I say oh, oh blend!
They say it's open
But I say it's now

Love is a sober house
Love is a sober place
Love is a sober church

They say rod and rod
I say he stays open
He heeds, he heeds, he heeds
He heeds me
He heeds and heeds my word
Love turns him
Love opens him, he is the one
But they say what? Who?
They say, is this he?
He is my purpose
He is my purpose
He is great, he *is* this

Love says, I blend the church
I blend the nation
Love says I blend this nation
They work, they work
They work to turn this
I say, it's day
It's time
Love is doing
For he is in me

They say oh God!
But I say he is
They say is this him?

I say yes it is him
He is the one in the rod
He is the one with the rod
The vote, the vote
They vote
It's now, it's day
It's now, it's day
I say who it is
Yes, and it is the one

LOVE IS A SONG

Love is a song
It's a song of purpose
It's a song of grace
It's a song of abundance
It's a song of the race

Love is a song
Love is a song of grace
Love is a word
For the father's great grace

Love is a time for the house to come
Love is a time for the church to come
Love is a time for the church to be
It is a time for things to be

Love is a time for the church to come
Love is a time for the church to be
For love is a time of great song
Love is a song for the church to sing

Love's a song for the nation to receive
And love is a song
That sings in the heart
For love is a love: blessing love

Love blendings, love blendings
Yes! Love blendings, love blendings
Yes, yes, yes, yes; yes, yes, yes, yes
Yes, yes, yes, yes, and yes!!

They say they say oh it's race
But I say blend, blend, blend, I say!
They say oh it's this, oh it's race
But I say it's time for the blend

It's now a blend I do for you
Oh now the nation, the nation
The nation is blend
It's blend-days
Yeah! It's blend-day

Oh time for me to blend!
Oh blend the nation
Oh blend the nation
Love is a blend and a song

Love is a blend and a song of songs
They say what word?
But I say it's a song
It's a song of grace

For the church—for your heart
It's a song of grace
Love says you sing
It says sing to me

It says God loves
None sing, none do
I do for you
I do for you

Love sings, love double
You sing, you see! You sing, you see!
Yes, you sing, you see!
God says love sings to the church

Love, love sings to the nation
Love sings to your house
Love sings to you and you
Love sings—you are mine!

LOVE IS A BLEND II

I say love blends things
But I say it's time to see
There's a great nation
There's a great change
There's a great love
There's a change in grace

Love blending, love blending
Yes, I love blending
I love blending nations
I love blending nations
There is them, there is them
Now there is them
Blending, blending
Blending, blending
Love says I am blending

Why do they say it's the race?
Why do they say it's his race?
Why they say it's his race?
But I say it's me, it's me!
They say oh no, not them!
I say yes, yes, yes, it's them!

They say oh the door, oh the door!
But I say come and come
They say now? Not now
I say love says now
Love says more and love says more
Love says yes! Yes!
Love says yes to this
And love says now I blend
The bold, the bold, the bold say yes

Love says my blend
It says blend, it says blend
Yes, it says blend!
It says the blend is now
And now is time
For now the blend is now time

Love says greater is this change
I say I do what I do, and I say
Love will turn what they say

WATER BLENDING

The water is blending
But the water is showing
The water is going and it's coming

It's the waters of power
It's the waters of love
It's love and it's love

God is showing
The mash, the mash
It's the great healing power

Love is as the waters of power

PATTERN

There's a pattern
It's a pattern of abundance
It's a pattern where
There's work and grace
Oh what is this pattern?
Oh it's a pattern of love

'Mazing, it's amazing
It's abundant blending
It's a blending of works
But it's a blending of love
It's a sharing, it's a sharing
It's an abundant work of grace

God's love is a great pattern
Yes, a great pattern
Greater, greater it is
It's a pattern of the least
It's a pattern of great
Oh it's a pattern of abundance

Oh it's a love pattern
It's a way of grace
It's a way of me
Oh but it's a way for thee
Rich, rich is this pattern
It's a pattern of man

It's a pattern for blessing
But it's a great pattern of visitation

The body
The body is a pattern
It's a pattern of the church
It's a pattern to show
But it's a pattern of love
Here the pattern

Here is the pattern
The pattern of nations
It's the pattern of blessing
But it's the pattern of least
It's the pattern of grace
Dorcas

Dorcas
Yes, you're to receive
Here is the one who stirs and stirs
Dorcas goes and receives the thing
Oh she does in this, this
Oh yes, the pattern

The pattern of abundance
Oh the pattern of love
Oh the pattern of healing
Oh the pattern
Heed and receive
The pattern for this day

Oh the pattern is me: it's me
Oh God says keep the pattern

WORDS OF LOVE

SECTION FIVE

NATIONS

LOVE IS A BRIDGE

Love is in a bridge
There is a bridge, and that is me
There is a bridge that you see
There is a bridge that comes into churches

There is a bridge for your nation
It's a bridge of great and great
It's a bridge into great things
It's a bridge to your grace

They're bringing, they're bringing
They are bringing them in
It's a great bridge
A bridge to great things

There's a blowing
But the bridge is stirring
It's stirring, but it's open
It's open to be, it's open to be

It's open to go
It's open to turn
It's open to stir-up
It's open to love-up

Love is as this bridge
Love is as this bridge
It's a bridge of abundance
But is a bridge to the nations
They say it's time to shut this bridge
It's time to close the bridge

I say
Open
Open
Open

THE GUARD

The guard!
The guard!
The guard is now
Bond, bond
Bond, bond
The guard?
Oh the guard!

It's a guard of grace
Motives?
It's of words and love
Words are guards
They guard your nation

Gate! Gates!
The gates of grace
I am cleansing the gates
The gate is now blessed
Blessed of me

Rumble, rumble
It's a rumble
It's a rumble
Love is a rumble
Rocky, it's rocky
But the word is the love
Love. Oh what is it?
It's rocky

IT'S LOVE

It's love, it's love
Say in the ear
Love is in, love is in
Say in the ear that love is in

Say, love and I love
Say in this
Say in that I love
I love this and I love them

Love brings in nations
You're to say
Love brings in nations
Love is the key

Love today
Love today
Love today
For now it's day

GOD-NATION

God-nation
Yes, God-nation
God-nation
Oh the nation of nations
Oh love's great blend!

LOVE WORD FOR THE SEED

They say, grown, grown, grown
They say we are grown
But I say you are seed
You are a seed, you are a seed today
They say oh we are?

Now I say, now is the day
Now is day, now is day—be!
Day to be my purpose
Day to be my purpose
Day to mercy

Day to me
Day to come
Day to me
It's a day of purpose
It's a day of me

Love says, seed, seed, seed—now!
It's seed in the church
It's seed in the nations
It's seed in the nations of purpose
It's seed in the house

Oh, oh, oh my seed!
I send you words, I send you words
And I send you change
Love says, love says
Love says, love says

Love says, now blown
I blow in the seed
They come—the seed
There is love I have for the seed
I love your seed, I love your seed

Love is now come for your seed
Double love! Double love!
And double love!
It's double love and double purpose
And love says seed works

Your seed works
They work, they work
They work and they work
They go to work
They go to the nations

They go to your nation
They go to the house
Love says, they be the change
They be the change
They 'be the one'

They be the one of grace
They be the one to be
They be the double
They be the one
Love says, they be the nations

They be the nations
They be the time
They are to be

FOR YOUR NATION

It's a word for the nation
Oh it's a word for the nation
It's a word for this nation

Oh days of wonders! Days of signs!
Days of abundance!
And days, days, that you receive!
Oh these are love-days

Days where you know my purpose
Days of love, days of love
Days these are, love-days
Days, love-days

You know my grace
Days of wonders, days of signs
Days of abiding and days I AM
Days you see, days you are

It's days of words
But it's days of abiding
Days I lead this nation
Days where blessings turn and are

Days where receiving is now
And days, God says, days you receive
Days of great turning to my grace
And great are the words you see

They say this nation
Oh this nation
But I say oh
This nation is abundant

This nation is open to me
Oh what days you see
They say this nation
Addled is this nation

I say this nation is blessed and blessed
And this nation is blessed of me
Oh what is this nation?
It's a great nation of nations

It's a nation of these!
It's a nation of these!
A nation of grace

A nation of grace
Oh nation
Oh nation
What are you?

Red, red, red, red
Words, words, word
You're red
You're red

You're with grace
You're red in blessing
You're red in my love
You're red in my blessing

You're white in blessing
You're white in me
You're white in love
And you're white in grace

You are blue in me
You are blue in blessing
You are blue in blessing grace
You are blue with abundance

You are blue, opening in me!
Blue in grace, love and love
You are blue in love-grace
And this nation will see open heavens

You're ready to be
You're ready to be
They say not now
They say this nation is not

They say this nation
Oh what is it now?
But I say it's a nation
Of great, great thing

THE LAD

The lad, oh who is this?
Oh who is the lad?
He is the one who is me
He is the one who is loved

The love here is the love for he
He's loved and he's loved
The blessed one is the blessed one
Here he is, here he is

In the moccasins, in the moccasins
He is great
He is loved and he is blessed
The love breach, the love breach

He is who I say: he is a great nation
He is a great church
You love this one
You love the one

Labor, labor, they do
They tote, they tote the burden
But I love to bless
I love to bless

I love him, I love they
They are my grace
They are my love
And they are my leaders

They are great, they are great
Late? Late? It is not
They are now abundant
For the lad is they, for the lad is they

RED BLOOD—RED MAN

There's red blood
It's red blood I love
Ready, ready, ready!
They're ready to come

It's red
The red blood
The red blood is now blessed
The red blood, the red blood
The red blood of this nation

Oh who are they?
These are they in need
Need of blessing
Red, the red man
Oh the one I receive

Oh the depths of operations
Oh the depths of wonders and signs
Oh the depths of love I see
Oh he is loved of me
He the one who is red

BRITAIN

Brit, Brit, Brit
It's Britain, Britain, Britain
It's Britain the grace, grace
Britain the place, it's Britain the grace

Oh Britain, oh Britain
Oh Britain, great, great, oh Britain
You are open, you are open
Oh Britain, God says now

God says now, grace
Oh grace, abundance of love
Oh grace, abundance of love
Oh love increase, love increase

Love increase, love work
They are open, they are open
Open Heaven, open Heaven
Oh God says Britain, Britain, Britain

Britain, Britain, Britain, Britain
God says Britain, oh great you are
Dad, dad, dad
God says dad is in Britain

The sod, the sod, the sod
The sod is abundant
The sod is abundant with great grace
Britain, the sod is open to me

The sod is open to heaven's grace
The sod is open to great
Great, great rain
The sod will open and receive

You will see love, love, love, love
The sod: open now!
The sod, yeah, the sod!
The sod operating

The sod operating
The love will turn
The love turns this house
The love turns this nation

Love is blessed; love I bless
Love is blessed and great is Britain
Dad, dad, they say where dad is?
They say rod, rod, rod, rod

But I say love, love, love, love
Live! Operate! Live! Operate!
I say Britain, love! Britain, love!
Ready, ready, ready for you!
Ready, ready, ready for you!

BATTLE FOR BRITAIN

It's time for this nation to open
God says, Britain I receive
Reside, reside, and I reside
Broad, broad and abroad

Ribbon, ribbon, ribbons of grace
The rocket, the rocket
It's time for operation: God in Britain
God says, Britain, watch this

Watch the grace, grace, grace
Rocket, rocket, rocket
For it's grace, grace, grace
The Maker is stirring
The Maker is stirring

DARK SEED

Yes, you are loved
God is lifting
Dad heeds, dad heeds
You are loved

Love hears the word
Love hears the words
Daddy's coming, daddy's coming
God loves the dark seed

God loves the dark
God loves the light
Yea he loves, yea he loves
Yea he loves
Dark...loved; dark...loved

Love is sending
He is lifting, lifting and lifting
The seed, the dark seed
The dark seed opens a great change

The dark seed is sharing
The dark seed hears things
The dark seed is lifting
Oh the dark seed lifts the church

Ways, ways, ways
Blend, blend, blend
God loves dark seed
God loves the blessing in the seed

The dark seed: great God loves things
God loves the many
The dads, the dads come and come
Oh dads are going to come

God loves these days
He loves, he loves, he loves
Dark seed, dark seed
God loves, he loves

Blending love
Blending love
It's time to be
It's time to be

Light, light, light
It's light for this seed
Oh there's light going and going
There's light in the church

Gold, gold these are
God is loved and God is loved
Loved here and loved here
It's time for grace and grace here
Write, write, God sending

God sending
It's time for these
The dark is daddy's blessing
Daddy's blessing opens Heaven

Oh Daddy's blessing opens grace
Oh Daddy's blessing opens grace
Oh Daddy's love is great in these
Bread, bread, bread

These are dark and they are loved
Dad loves, he loves these
Watch, watch, watch, lift
Watch and see

Raised, raised, raised this day
God loves, he loves, he loves
Love is in this great, great, seed
There's a work on this blessed seed

The seed is healed
The seed is working
The seed is joining
The seed is hearing

Dark Seed - (continued)

Raising, raising great churches
The love is in this one
He's loving, he's loving
He's loved for he is my grace

Rise, seed, rise
Rise to rest
Rise to know
And rise to be

Love opens today
It's time to be
It's time to have
Oh it's time to shed

Oh it's time to blend
It's time to tend
It's dad and dad
Oh dad loves the dark seed

It's a lift, it's a lift
Lift and lift this change
Lift I do, lift I do
Oh daddy is in this

ARABS

Arabs, Arabs, Arabs
Oh I see
Oh I do receive
The word is: operation

Oh the ones of work
The ones who work
They say, oh I do not see
But I know I see

I know I see
But I know, I do
I see, I love
I love these, I love these

These Arabs I love
I love to abundantly bless
They I love
I love these, I love these

They say bit, bit, bit
The bit, the bit
I say, you are blessed, blessed, blessed
They are my blessing

These, the Arabs
They are my blessing
These Arabs are 'what?' they say
They are loved, blessed, loved and
Loved, loved, and loved!

They are now abundant
They are abundant in grace
Raising them, raising them
Raising them to know
Raising them to be

To be of my grace
They are my grace
My grace of love
My grace of healing

They are loved and blessed
They are loved, oh what loved!
They are abundantly loved
They are loved and abundant

Hagar, Hagar, Hagar
Loved, loved and loved!
Your son: loved! Loved! Loved!
He's loved! He's loved!

Loved! Just rest in it
Love, you are to receive
Oh they will see
They will receive

Oh they will know
Oh, oh watch they will know
They will know my blessing
They will see my abundance

They will have my abundance
But they will shed this
They will shed that
Oh they will shed things
They will shed odd things

They will shed old things
They will know the grace
They say, it's in this, it's in that
They say it's merit
They say merit is blessing

Arabs - (continued)

But it's grace
They will see love, love
They will know I love
They will see my love

Raid, raid, raid, they raid
But I send grace, grace, grace
They see grace, grace, grace
Love is going to turn them

Love will open their nation
Love will turn their nations
Love will heal them

They say bit, bit, bit
Mutt, mutt, mutt
They say odd, odd, odd
But I say they are loved, loved, loved

They are abundant in grace
They are abundant in love
And now they are abiding
They are in me; they are in me

IRAN

Iran, Iran, Iran
They say you are utter, utter, utter
But the turn, the purpose
They say old is this, old

A great open heaven in this nation
Iran, Iran, they say Iran
I say it's a time for they to see
A time for them to know

Blessing of my purpose
Iran is a place of abiding power
God says it's a place
Of abundant purpose
It's a place for my grace to turn

It's Iran's time
It's Iran's time for grace
It's Iran's time for the power
It's Iran's time
For commands to come

But I send what I send in
It's time they see that
I-AM-THAT-I-AM
They are to see that
I-AM-THAT-I-AM
God says it's Iran's time for me

They will see great power
They will see blessing of grace
They will see my blessing
They will see my grace

It's day, it's day, oh it's day
It's day for Iran, it is day in Iran
They say this in that?
But it is day in this place

For now they will know who I am
They will know that I AM
They will know this is the way
And they will know I am the way

ABOUT JEWS

They say the Jews are this
But I say I see
They say what are they?
I say they are my purpose

But they say they are not
I say they are in purpose
Oh they say these, these, these!
I say watch, watch

But I say they are open to me
Love them...love them
They say gun these! Gun them!
And purge! Purge! Purge!

I say they are my, my, my purpose
They say battle them
I say oh I turn this
They say turn them up
Turn them up, up, and out

But I say love is in them
Love says visit them
They say done are they
I say I visit them...but
I will turn them to my blessing

LOVE IS AN ART

Love is an art
Love is an art of grace
Love is an art of me
Love is an art of thee!

Art is an art for these
Love is an art of arts
An art of love is an art of sharing
It's an art to be, it's an art to see

Love is an art you do and see
Love is an art
Oh it's an art of growing
It's an art for great sharing

Love is an art for couples
It's an art for churches
It's an art for blessing
It's an art form of me

It's white and red and black
It's whites and reds and blacks
It's they who come to see
It's they who see I am in they!

Love is art, for they will know
Love is art; love is a blend
Love is a great art
Love is a great art to do

They say oh it's a shade
Love is my grace
Love is a great art of grace I send
Great shades of love, oh
Love is a great, great, great, shading

The red, the red, the red
The red, oh I love these
The red, oh I love the red
The red, who are in the nation
Oh I love to turn them to me
They are opening to me
Oh they are my love
The love I send

I love to love the white
The white, the white, the white
The whites who are of this nation
The whites they are come to me
They are to come to me
They are open to me
And I turn these to me

Oh they who are the black
Oh they are—oh I love
Oh the black I love
Oh the love I have for these
It's love, love, love
Love I have for these
I love to turn these to me

The love is in these
Love is a love of these
Love is a great, great art
Love is a mat of great art
Love is a mat of color
It's a mat of colors of love

LOVE LEAPING

I love leaping
Yes, I love to leap
Yes, I love to show
Yes, I love to receive

It's love
It's love and love
It's love, love
It's love, my love

I love you
Yes, I love you
Yes, oh yes
Oh yes, oh yes
Oh God loves, yes

Oh God loves and loves
Yes, God loves and loves
He loves and he loves
He loves, oh how he loves!

God loves
He loves you and you
He loves you and you
Yes, oh yes

The racist
Oh how is it he is?
He's a debt, a debt on the nations
Oh he's a debt in the church

God is love
He is love
He is love for nations
He loves and loves
He loves
The
Nations

THE NOBLES

The noble, the nobles
They are sent to change nations
They are the nobles
Who are they? Who are they?

They are leaders, they are leaders
They are leaders of love
Funds and funds they send
Funds they send to the nations

Love is sending these
Oh love is sending these
Oh love is sending these
Love is these

LOVE IS A MEND

Love is a mend
Oh what is a mend?
Love is a mend of nations
Love is a mend
Oh great mantles, mend!
Love is a mend of nations and nations
Love is a mend of great nations
Love is a word
But it's me!

WORDS OF LOVE

SECTION SIX

GRACE

BODY GRACE

Limit, limit, limit, they say
God is abundant and great here
Lady, lady, operate grace
Body grace, body grace

The house
The church is in body grace
Matters of visitations
Matters of words

Dine in blessings
And dine in purpose
Ready for this?
Ready for me?

Many grace, many grace
A diamond: love, love
Blessing love, blessing grace
Hop, hop and great grace

Love says abundant grace
God is dad, God is dad
The ribbons of visitation
The least will see grace

Grace operates here and there
But now grace is now
Now, now for these
Daddy hears, daddy loves

Daughters, sons are now
Daughters, sons are now

GOD IS GREAT IN GRACE

God is abundant
And God is great
God is love
God is great

It's God-love, it's God-love
God is love here and love yes
God hears and God loves
God is a great answer

Love is great and love is me
Ladies, ladies, God's love
Ladies, ladies, God does love
Love for these, love for these

Love hears and love comes
Dad's love is that I send
Rest and love; it's a love of grace
It's a love of love

There's a battle for grace
God's secret is in grace
Lady Grace, it's Lady Grace
My grace is love

Dad's sharing, dad is sharing
Love is abundant—for it's me
Love operates here…there
Love operates here and there

LOVE OPERATES

It operates, it operates
It operates in blessing

They say luck
But I say blessing
I say blessing is in me
I say blessing is in me
They say oh it's in this, doing this
I say it's in my grace
I say it's in my grace

I say grace is the key
The key to abundance
The key to open heavens
The key to abundance of grace
The key to the work of grace
The key to great blessing
The key to 'the secret'

The key to blessing
The key to grace
It's the key to opening, opening
The key to abundance
The key to open visitations
The key to generations
The key to receiving

They say it is in luck
But it is in me

DOUBLES!

Doubles! Doubles! Doubles!
It's double abundance
It's double answers
It's double love

Operations of grace
And operations of healings
And operations of love
Oh what love! Oh what love!

It's double! It's double! It's double!
Double God and double growing
Double abundance and double grace
I send double: oh, oh double

It's double cups, it's double grace
It's double need, but it's double seed
My, my, my, what double!
Oh double wonders, oh double love

Daddy, daddy says double, double
There's a double change
There's a double cup
It's a cup of signs and grace

It's a double cup of
Signs and abundance
The diamond double
It's blessings and grace

The diamond double
Is grace and blessing
Oh what doubles!
Oh double love, double grace

Love is double
Double, double
Love is blessed
Love is double

SHEPHERDING

There's a shepherding
They're shepherding
They say it's this, it's that
They say to be, to be

I say my grace, my grace
I say abundance, grace
Abundant grace, the shepherding
You will see the shepherding

They say it's in me you're to be
They say you're to be old and in me
You're to be this, you're to be that
But I say you are in grace
You are in me

Daddy, daddy, daddy
You're to shed! You're to shed this
The shepherding, the shepherding
They're to shed

They say, thing is to be
I say God is great: grace is me
They say don't do, don't do
But I say you are

God says it's grace, grace
They say add this, add that
I say grace blessing, grace blessings
They say generation, do this
They say sit, sit, you're to sit now

I say God is open, God is open
Oh the shepherd, oh the shepherding
Oh the shepherding
Oh the shepherd

They're going to do
But there's you
You're going to be
Love is a great thing to be

IT'S GRACE!

It's grace, it's grace, it's grace!
Oh it's diverse grace
Blessing and blessing
My grace is broad
And my grace is love
My grace, oh what is it?

Oh what grace!
Oh it is grace to know
To know my abundance
It's grace to know
My abundant blessing
My grace works in the man

Grace is increased in he
Grace is vision to be
And grace is abundance of healings
Grace is abundance of works blessing
But grace is me…and me in you!
Blessing in thee
And blessing to receive

LEAP UP!

You're to leap up
God says leap up
Leap into my grace
Leap into me
Leap into grace

Leap, oh love's great leap
The leap into abundance
The leap into growing
The leap into change
The leap is to tell

VISIT

God says visit
Oh it's me
It's me who comes
It's me who visits
It's me who comes to see
It's me who comes to say
It's me who loves to say
God is saying it's me who comes

Dance, dance and dance in me
Ride, ride in my power
Oh leap and love
It's today a visit

THERE'S A SIGN

There's a sign; it's a sign
The sign of grace
The sign of blessing
The sign of days

The sign of bread
And the sign of blessing
The sign of abundance
The sign of answers

The water, the water
The water is open
It's the waters of abundance
The waters of showers

The sign of my grace
The sign of my blessing
The sign of things to be
Oh it's the sign of my power

Daddy, daddy-God is in this
Oh days, oh days, days of grace
This day is grace, this day is grace
Blessing words, blessing hours

THE WOMB

Womb, womb
Womb, womb
Love is in this
It's in the womb

The nut, the nut
The nut says no
They say oh that is not
But I say this is grace

Grace and grace is in the womb
What they do, what they do
They say oh, oh, oh cut this
I say love is in this

I say love is in this
Love is in this womb
Love is in this
Love of grace

Love of words, love of love
Love is answering in this
Love is answering in this word
Love is in the womb

WHY THE BLOOD

Why the blood?
Why the blood?
They say why the blood?
The blood is blessing
The blood is increased
The blood is wonder
The blood is healing
The blood is blessed
The blood is a dream
It is the blessing of my grace
It is the blessing of the church

WORDS OF LOVE

SECTION SEVEN

GOD'S VARIETY STORE

THE CROW

The crow, the crow who is not
The crow, oh the crow is not
Dust he comes in, dust comes in
The crow bad, the crow is bad

He says you're not
The crows says you're not
Love says you are
He says you are abundant

Bad, the crow is, he's bad
He's a burden
The burden of words
The burden he says

The burden he says
The burden of teasings
The burden of gossip
He's a burden

He's a burden, but he's here
He's to be taught I AM
He's to be taught love is
He's to be taught dad loves

He's to be sent out
He's not my grace
Oh he is not my love
He is not here, he is dead

Love is great, he's love
Love is me, he...I AM
I AM love, I AM love
Love opens abundance

God is abundant: he is great
God is love, yes God is love
The boasting—Not!
The boasting—Not!

I am great, I am abundant
Love is great and love is a love
Amazing to be
Amazing to receive

It's great love
It's great love
Love is a great leap
A great leap to blessing

Blessing loves
He loves to bless
He loves to grow
He loves to grow

Love is a blessing
For blessings now

THE ROACH

The roach can
The roach is
The roach does
The roach hears

The roach works
The roach blesses
The roach changes
But the roach blesses

The roach loves to show
The roach loves to receive
The roach grows here
The roach grows there

The roach is a blessing
The roach is dad's visitation
The roach is dad's grace
The roach is a great power

He's a great, great blessing
He's a working power
He's a great sign
He's a love-show

The roach is the great blessing
He is the blessing in the city
He's the blessing in the house
He's the blessing in your nation

He's a great abundance
He's a sign, he's a sign
Oh he's a sign for the church
He's a sign of love's blessing

He's a sign unto open doors
Working, working
Abundant workings
Love opens things now

But now it's time for this to come
For it's time for this to be
It's time for the roach to show
It's time for this to come

BIRD IS A BIRD

Bird is a bird
He is a bird
He's here, he's there
He is in that, he is in that
He's a bird, he's a bird

The bird commands
And the bird turns
The bird sees and the bird turns
It's the bird: the bird abides
He abides, he abides
He abides in purpose

I love this one, I love the bird
Why, they say, he does, he does?
He is who he is, he is the bird
The bird is love the bird loves
He loves, he loves to see
The bird, he loves to be

He opens, and he sees
He sees things
He sees a place, he sees a house
He sees that the door opens
He sees the door opens, he comes in
He sees things in the place
He sees, but he sees the old
He sees them in this
He sees them in that
He sees that they are in that
He sees that is the cut

They cut them, they cut the old
They cut the man who is the purpose
They cut this, they cut that
They cut leads of my grace
They cut the man
They cut the *on*
They cut the word
They cut the power
They cut the word
They cut the power

They cut me
They cut me
They cut me!
Yes, they cut me!
The word is me

It's me that is the bird
Love me
Love my purpose
Love me
For I am the purpose
Love is me for I am the one

He is the bird
The bird comes to the church
He comes to see
The bird comes to the church
To do and be
Love, love, the bird says

They say, bird, bird
This is a turd!
They say this is tough
Love is the utter this
They say it's old
They say, oh this? No!
They say no to me
They say no to me
But I go, I go on
I go to a house
I go to see

I go to see where it is
There will be a place for my purpose
There will be a house of grace
A house for me to be

LEMONS

Lemons, lemons
Lemons, they say
They say lemons!
They say oh lemons!
They say oh this is lemons!

But, but I say, it is blessing
It's blessing for abundance
It's blessing for abundance
For abundance
It's blessing for abundance, for grace

It's grace that turns a lemon
It turns a lemon to blessing
They say lemon, lemon
What lemon!
But I say love turns it to blessing

Love is the door of the lemon
It's the door to grace
It's the door to love
And it's blessing

It's love that blesses the love
It's love that blesses the love
For it's love that turns it
For it's love that turns it
To grow and be a blessing

God asks…
Why do they say lemons?
Why they say it is that?
I say it is abundance
Into a great power

He says now I turn the lemon
I turn the lemon to finance
I turn the lemon to healing
I turn the lemon to grace
I turn it to blessings

THE NUT

They say it's the nut
It's the nut who sees my grace
It's the nut they say
But I say it's me

They say, oh this is the nut
But they say oh this is not me
But I AM blessing
I AM abundance, I AM healing

God says who is he?
He is, he is and he is
He is the Word

IT'S A DIAMOND

The diamond—oh where is it?
It's in these, it's in these
And it's in these, oh it's in these

Oh the diamond is grace
It's a great show of me
It's a show of my abundance
It's a show for these

You are in me
You are in my purpose
Love is in you—it's a diamond!

It's wearing in you
It's wearing in thee
It's wearing in grace
It's wearing in love

Diamond, diamond
Diamond brings grace
Diamonds raise blessings

It's diamonds that bless the nation
But diamonds are in thee

GOLD! IT'S GOLD!

They say where is it?
Gold! Where?
I say it's in houses
It's in churches

It's in the nation
It's in the nation
Gold! Gold!
Oh great gold!

Oh gold in things
Gold in blessings
There is a gold rush
But it is in the church

I'm blowing in gold
They ask what is this in the church?
This is a certainty…
But it is me!

It's me, opening the heavens
It's me, opening the church
It's me, loving my house
It's me, abundant! Abundant!

Oh they say, but where?
It's a blowing wind
Oh a blowing wind!
What wind? What wind?

It's my power, it's my blessing
It's my visitation, it's my love
There's great love
Great love—visit

It's great love
Oh blessing love
Oh what love!

THE DIAMOND

The diamond blessing

There's a diamond
There's a diamond working
Why, oh why, the words are come?
The diamond is the word
The diamond is blessing
Love is a diamond
Oh but it's
Great

Love is a diamond
Opening in grace
Love is a diamond
Opening in blessing

Love is as a diamond
Growing and open
Love is as a diamond
Oh what words!
They are words of works
They are words of grace

They are words of great abundance
And they are words of
Abundant power

THESE DOORS OPEN

This is a door, this is a door
This door is open
This door opens and you go
The doors, the doors
Oh these doors are open

These doors of blessings
These doors of abundance
These doors of blessings
These doors of abundance
These doors of operation

THUNDERS, THUNDERS THUNDERS

Thunders, thunders, thunders
It's the blessing
They say what is that?
I say oh what is that?
It's the sound of blessing
What sound?
What sound is that?
Oh the sound of wonders
The sound of love
The sound of healing
The sound is love

RALLY

Rally, rally, rally
It's a rally for blessing
A rally for love
It's a rally each day
It's a rally to go
It's a rally for God
It's a rally
Word, word, word!

BUT IT'S IN THE BLUE

They say oh it's blue
I say oh it's my power
My power to turn it
My power to turn a key

It's power to turn a key
It's power to turn the key to a place
It's power to turn the key to a house
It's power to turn a house

It's power to open a house
It's power to turn and do
It's power for a city
It's power for a city
It's power for the cars

It's power for them to go
But it's power for this day
It's power opening
It's power for the car

It's power that will turn this nation
It's power, it's power, I turn
But it's in the blue
But it's in the blue

ABUNDANCE OF POWER

There's a great thing: it's burning
It's burning! It's burning up!
They say what is this?
It's abundance of power

It's an abundance of power
What is this they say?
They see this
But they say what is this?

Oh they say this is the key
The key to the power
The power for a house
They say it's a great thing

But it's the power to turn a house
It's power to turn a church
It's power to turn a nation
They're making this for this day

They say for it's today for this day
They say oh it will turn this nation
It will turn the key
They say it's a stirring up of blessing

The motor, the motor?
They will have a motor!
For it's a motor for this thing
For it's in the blue

They say 'wrap this'
I say it is for now
The battle, the battle for this is now
But I say it's time
It's time for this to be

THE MIGHTY MIGHTIES

The Mighty Mighties
What are they?
These who stand
The Mighty Mighties

They are answers
They are blessings
They are mantles
They are great in the house

The masters of grace
The martyrs they are
They are abundant in blessing
God is working in them
...blazing grace

GOD-MAN

It's God-man, it's God-man
Oh who is the God-man?
He is the word
He is the word

He is my word
He is—oh me!
He is my seed
He is the one

But he is in this
Oh he is come, he is come
He is come to the church
He is come to say

He is come today
He is come—oh he comes
He says, he says
I come, I come, I come today

I come to be, I come to turn
I turn…receive!
I turn this house
I turn the church

Why, why, why you do this?
Why, why do you that?
Love says now is the day
Love says now!

And love says open!
Oh love says where, where, where
And where, where and where
And where is this?

Where is that?
It is I who is that
It is I who is this
It is I who is that

It is I who opens
It is I who heals
It is I who comes
It is I who comes and comes to you

Oh my, my, why do you do?
Why do you know what to do?
For it is I who is
Who is this, who is that!

Who is the door, who is the door!
Oh, oh, oh more, more
More, more to see
It's more, more for you to see

Now for you to receive, for I AM
For I, it's I who is, who receives you
I receive you, I say, yeah!
I say yeah, now I say yes now

I say now come, I say now, now
I love: love increases me
I say love loves me
I say love blends things

SPEED WORDS

These are speed words
Guns, guns, guns
Guns, guns, guns
Are they this? Are they that?

What are they?
They are for them
These are for them who say
It is dead

Love says it is day for you to see
It is day for you to be
It says watch
I AM WHAT I AM

They say it's dead
I say a great change
They say brat, brat, brat
But I say here is me

They say dumb is this
But I say what they are is abundant
They say boy is he this
But I say he is my power

They say what is this?
They say who is this?
I say he is loved
And I say they are loved

COME OUT!

Come out, come out, come out
Come out and come out
It's time to come out
It's dumb to do this
Dumb is dumb
Dumb is dumb
It's dumb to say
It's time for this gun
It's day to come to me
They say it's the gun
I say it's dumb

It's time for abundance
It's time for blending
It's time for abundance
It's time for the blend
Lay this to my purpose
It's time for blessing
It's time for purpose

They say it's done
I say it's abundant
They say not this!
I say it's me!
Love today will blow a house
Love is here, love is in me
Love, love opens a heart
It's love that opens a place
It's love that opens a heart
Love is a blend, it blends a church
Love is a top, it tops things

GUNS OR LOVE

They say it's the guns
I say it's me
They say it's day
It's time for the guns
Love says it's now time for me

They say oh day! It's gun-day
But I say it's now me!
But they say oh this we need to do
The time to do this
They say come now!

It's this now
It's time to turn to it
I say love, love, love, love!
They say love is a butt of this
But I say love is power

DANGER! DANGER!

They say danger, danger!
Danger to do, danger to be
They say don't do and do and do
They say no, not that!
They say don't go there!

They say it's there for this
They say it's not this day
They say oh the danger
I say oh the love
They say oh God, oh God!

I say yea, yea!

THE BODY

They say the body is changed
And the body is shedding
I say the body is abundant
The body is abundant

The body is the answer
And the body is here
They say the body is cut
They say the body, the body is not

Desert, desert
It's time for desert
Love is blessed in the body
It's an operation on the body

SHARE IT

Share it, share it
It's things, it's works, it's blessing
Oh it's a great thing to show
Oh it's sharing and sharing

You're to share love and grace
Share love and share abundance
God shares, God shares
God shares…he is

He is who he is
He shares, he's love
Yes, share love, share blessing
God says show, show

God is great in great sharing
It's time to be
For it's time to share

THE PAST

My, my, my
Oh they say what was! Oh what was!
They say not now
But I say love is in this

They are saying odd these days
Blessing cut, they say blessing cut
They say this is for they
Oh they say it's for they and they

My God is abundant
This day is great days
They say this is not now
This is not for now

But I say now and now
Oh it's now, and it's for now
Blessing brings blessing
They say the abased are to be

I love this, I love they
The days are abundant
Lazy are they?
They say lazy
God is great and God comes in

Love purpose, love grace
Oh love, it's time for them
Oh love blesses these
God is great and God is blessing

God is great and he is abundant
They say it's not day for this
Blessing for this they say
Blessing for you, but blessing for they

I do, I see
It's time for blessing
It's time for abundance
They say they are not to be

Blessing is now open to receive
Mad, mad, mad
They are old and mad
Who say not now

Days of this, oh not this
They say the days of this
They say oh the days of old
I turn this time

I turn the times, I turn the times
Oh it's time for the grace
The grace for nations
The time for grace in nations

It's time for blessing, blessing
The naked will receive
The naked will be
Oh blessing to have
Oh blessing to receive

The now is the now
There's a force for grace
There's a force for blessing
But there's a force for the ones

The force here for these
It's time to do
It's time to have
Its time to have my grace, my love

The Past - (continued)

They say oh the days
They say oh the days of this
But it's this day
My grace

The mad they are
The mad they are
It's time to be
Blessing to receive

It's the maker's thing
The maker's show
It's the maker's day
It's the maker's time

Blending yea, blending
I make nations blend
Dark and light
Dark seed, light seed

The blend I do
The blend I do
They say bad is this
Now is the day for this blend
Blending, blending it's going to be

It's being, it's being
It's being open to me
What is this, what is that?
Mining, mining, mining

The mining of grace
The mine is blessed
The mine is blessed
It's the day to be...the day to do

THIS IS A ROCKET GENERATION

What is it?

It's soaring into my grace
It's soaring into my grace
It's going to be the generation
It's going to be the great generation

Oh it's a generation of healing
It's a generation of blessing
It's a generation of blending
It's a generation of open visitation

A ripe grace, yes, it's ripe
It's a ripe blessing
It's a ripe blending
It's a ripe peace

There's a rich leaping
There's a rich grace
There's a rich more
There's a rich blending

Rocket, rocket
This is the one
The rocket is now
It's the rocket, opening and doing

ROCKET

Rocket, rocket, rocket
Oh you see this rocket?
This rocket is abundant
Ride, ride, ride; ride this now

Ride this rocket to abundant power!
This rocket is power
My power to turn
Oh my power on the church
Power! Oh great power to turn

It's a great ride, great ride
It's a ride on me
It's a ride you are on me
A ride to the nations

Oh prophesy the nations
Oh prophesy the nations
Oh the nations, it's time
Oh this rocket
It is a rocket of my grace

Oh it's a rocket of great power
It's a great blast, blast, blast-off!
It's time to turn, it's time to be
It's time to be in mission
It's a blast, blast, blast, you're on!

WORDS OF LOVE

SECTION EIGHT

LOVE IS

LOVE IS...

Love is old they say
But now, it's day
Run and run and run in this
Run and run for this is day

Love, love, love now
Love, love, love this now
Love, love, love them now

Love is a time and now it's time
Love is a time and now it's time
Love is an hour, for now it's time
Love is a word, but now it's time

Love is open for the house
Love is a house that is open to me
Love is a more of purpose

And love is an utter love
And love is an honor to do and see
And love is an honor to be and see

Love is a blessing, it is a purpose
Love is a mantle, it is a purpose
Love is a word they say in the nation
And love is a healing in the church

And love is a word
You see in the church
Watch—need, watch—need
Watch. Need. Watch. Need

Love is a neighbor
Who's in your church?
Love is a more, more of my grace
Love is a meeting where I AM

Love is more, more
More of my power
Love is one who comes to me

Love is a seed
In the hand of the sower
Love is a word…but it is me
Love is a word…but it is me

Love is healing, love is money
Love is the seed that comes to this
Love is a heart that's in my blessing

And love is a one
Who's loved of them
Love is a dent in the heart

Love is a cut
A cut in the heart

BLESSED LOVE

This love is me, this love is me
It's love of man; it's love of these
It's love of the church
It's love of the mighty
For it's love of my blessings
Oh great is my grace!

LOVE IS A HEALING

It's love
Love is a healing
Healing the church
Healing the leaders
Love is a healing and it's a great
healing

IT'S A LOVE HEALING

Love is a healing
It heals you to do
Love heals you to receive
Love heals you to know me
Love heals you to do in me

LOVE IS A BLESSING

Love is a blessing
It's a blessing to receive
Love is a blessing
A blessing to see
Love is a word
Oh love is me!

LOVE THOUGHTS...

Love loves secrets
It's secrets today
Love secret, love secret
Oh yes, love secret I send

Love months, love months
These are love months

Mutt! Mutt!
They say it's the mutts
God says, I love the mutt
It's love for the mutt

They say love is a gun
But it is me
They say love is a gut
They say love is a-uh??
They say love is dumb
They say love is old
They say love is an opera
God says love is me

Love is a candle

Love is a joy
A great, great thing
Joy is joy, but it is me!

Love is about grace
It's grace in me
But love, love, love…is me!

They say it's a zerbert
But I say it's what I send
I send the words of love and healing
I send love words to the nations

I open the mantle
There's love in the mantle
There's love in the mantle
And there's love in me

Love is the blowing wind
And love is in a great blustery wind
They say love is a wind
Oh, oh, oh, but love is in me!

Love is a word blowing a church
Love is a word that blows in a house

They say love is a blending
God says I'm blending
Love says I'm blending
Love blesses
Love is a great joy
Love is a great lazy
Love's as a dream in my grace
They say love is a dream

They say love is a dud
They say love is a great dud
But I say love is a great blessing
It's a great blessing

They say love is dead
I say love is open
They say love was a thing
Of times that were

I say love is in this day
I say love is for this day
They say it's old
I say it's now

Love Thoughts - (continued)

They say generation
That says this is not
They say dumb they are
They say this and that
About this change
Done they are, done they are
But I say they are open to me
I say what they are is mine

Love is opening this nation
Love is opening this house
Love is here and love is now

Love is loving, loving, loving
And love is loving these and them
What are they open to they say
But I say love is open to these

It's loving, but it's receiving
It's loving, and I receive
Love is a work, but it's me
Love is a work, but oh
What it is, is me

Watch your love
Yes, watch who you see
Mighty, mighty joy comes
Joy now, receive

Duck, for it comes
Duck, for it comes
Oh duck, but it comes
Oh let the door open
You're to let me in

They say the nap
They say it's a nap in this house
But I say it's day to awake
They say it's time for a nap
But I say it's time to awake
Oh it's time, for I say it's time

Loves says dream dreams
And have visions
Have the vision, have the vision
Have the vision

Love is word
Love is the mantle
Love is the mantle you receive
When you pray

Love is a secret
For it is a secret of the church
Love is a secret
For it's a secret of the nation

They are saying man who is this?
But I say love is in the church
They say blood, but I say love
They say it's the door, you go

But love opens a place
Love opens a grace
Oh they say the door!
It's time to go
Love says it's a day of grace
They say love is a secret
But oh love is me!

Love Thoughts -(continued)

Lover, lover, lover
They say it's a word
But what is a word?
Love is a changer
Who sees and grows

Love is a sup
It is a sup of my words
It is a sup of my grace
They say love is a blessing, it is me

Love is a need that you receive
Love is a need
But you know that I AM

Love is a blessing
And abundance is a church

Joy is a joy—great joy
It opens you to me

Love is a gun
They say love is a gun
Love is my word
Love is power
Love is bringing nations and nations

Love is a need
But it's a blessing
Love is a need
But it's a blessing—receive!

The budding
These are budding
The budding of power and power
These are buddings of a great day
These are love secrets I tell you
Love is a love, but it is a seed-bud
It's a budding seed
It's a budding love

As you dare it—you receive it
As you dare, you receive
As you see, you know
As you love, you receive

LOVE IS A WORD

Love is a word to them
But it's a purpose
And it's me

Love is loving many
I love to turn this to me
This is love: it's love to be

Love is work
It's a work of command

I LOVE, BUT...

Love word, love word
The word is but
They say love...but
But I say love here, love yes!

I say love here, love there
Love now, love then
Love here and love there
Love now, love then

Love here and love them
They say love now?
Yes, love now!
They say love this?
Love them? Love this?

They say why?
What? They say why?
For I say, it is
And I say it's now

For I say it's word
And I say it's abundant
Love says yes and love says here
Love says it is and it is, and it is

They say love is not
They say love is here
But they say love is not
They say love is for this
But I say love is for them

They say it's for me
But I say yes, it is!
I say for you *and* them
It's for them, for them
For you, for them

There's great love
For months and months
Love, love, love is great you see
Love, increase love, increase
Oh the love is increased!

Oh what love comes today!
Oh it's great for them, I say
Love is a man who says it is
And love is a man
Is a man who says it is

For God is love and love is me
Love is in me
Love is in me
Love is a need

Love is a seed
Love is a seed—what you sow
Love is a seed that comes in the heart
And love comes now in the heart

A WORD YOU LOVE TO BE

Love is a word
You love to be
Blessing, blessing
Open heaven
Love is a word—odd they say
But it is a word to see and receive

And love blesses
Love blesses and adds
Love blesses and sheds
Love blesses and changes

Love blesses and love is a secret
Love is an operation here
Love is an open-heart operation

Love is a she who is with a he
Love is a she and a he
Love is the seed they see
Love is the seed of the seed

WORDS AND LOVE

Words work, words work
There is a word that works
Words work…they work to provide
Love works…it works in the house

Love is a word that blesses a house
Love increases a place and a house
Love is a word in the ear
It's the ear in the ear
It's the ear in the ear
Yea, love the word is the word

The ear is in the word
The ear is in you
Love in the word and love in the ear
Love oh love, love is the word

Love is a word, but it's my power
It's my power to go
It's my power to be
It's my power of abundance
It's my power of healing

It's love, old days they say
Love is now in today
For love will turn
Love will turn a house, a church
Love will turn a church to grace

Love is utter love to me
Love is a word they say
Love is a power, a power to say
Love heals you to me. I see

Love is a love to receive in me
Love loves you
Love…heed me
Love…see me

Love is I
Love loves things
Love is a set
It's a set of abundance
It's a set—a set to see
It's a done grace, you see

Love loves to be
Love, oh you are ready
Love, you are ready to be
Love! I do

LOVE WORDS

Love words are a love purpose
For it's love to them
Love is things to them
But it's love, love I send to them

Oh I send them this day
It's the word of God
It's the word of God
It's the word of God
…it's the word of God

LOVE IS A GREAT SHUDDER

Love is a great shudder
Arrested, arrested, arrested
Arrested in my grace

LOVE BEAT

Love beat
Oh the beat of my grace
Love is a beat on your heart
Love is a beat God says he sends

Love is a beat
But it is a beat of grace
Love is beating in things and things
And love is a beat, beat, beat

Love is a beat
Opening your nation
Love is a great sound
Love is a sound

Love is a beat
God says see my beat
You're a beat
You're MY beat!

LOVE IS A CHANGE

Love is a change
It's a change opening
Oh love is a great ear
Love is a great he, love is a great she

Love is hearing
And love is hearing this, hearing they
Love says it's an abasing this
Love, love is a job of grace

LOVE BEATS

Mighty blessing, mighty blessing
Oh the beats are opening up
Oh the beats of my grace
And my change
The beat is the beat of grace
The beat is the beat of man
Oh the beat is the beat of blending
Love is a beat and love is a beat
Oh love is a great heart in grace

But love is a beat for your nation
And love is a great beat
Here and there
Oh love is a great sound
And a sound in grace

The heart is a beat of my grace
The heart beats in me, in me
Oh the heart beats in blessing love
And daddy and these are a beat

Blending, oh the blending
Oh the blending of more and more
My love beats, my love beats
Yes my love beats here and now
Dad oh dad
Whose heart beats for his house
Oh his heart is a great one
Oh the love he has here
Oh the love is great, and a great love

The beat is in his heart
Oh the beat is in he
Oh pop, oh pop!
Oh pop is come!

The love is in the heart
The beat here
The beat in here

LOVE LANE

It's love lane
It's love lane
Yeah! It's love lane
Yes, love, love
Love lane is a purpose
Love lane is a heart

Love lane is a heart
It's a place
Love is a place
It's a heart
Love is a heart
It's a place
Love, oh love is a place
Love, a place of the heart
Love!
A place is in a heart

IT'S THE BRIDE

It's the bride, it's the bride!
Yes, yes, yes, yes!
Oh! Oh! Oh yes!
Oh! What is this?
It's my answer! It's my bride!

Light! There's light
There's light on this
There's a light on my bride
The light is a light of grace
It's a new thing: great grace

Oh love, I do say on this who is
This is the purpose
Oh it's me! Oh yes!
It's raising a thing
It's raising a house, it's raising a one

They say this is not
I say God is in this
It's my bride, it's my bride
Yes! Yes! It's my bride!
They say this is the cut

They say it's to see, it's to see in
They say it's to turn things
I say love will turn it
Love is the key into my bride
It's the key to blessing the one

The word says: love is the key to me
The key to growing
Love is the power in the church
Love is the power in the bride

LOVE IS A FUSS

Love is a-fussing
It's a-fussing in the place
Love is a-fussing…yea a day
Love is a-fussing…an old love

Love is a-fussing, oh it fusses
Oh it fusses in the church
Love is a fuss
It fusses in houses

LOVE IS A LOCATION

Love is a location
It's a house
Love is a house, where I am
Love is a place of man
It's a place for him
It's a place for him to be
It's a place for him to receive
It's a place for him to know
That I AM
It's a place of command
It's a place of purpose
Love is a place for my purpose
They say the love
But they love in words
Man loves in words
But he loves for this, for this
God says love is power
It's power in purpose
It's power in grace
Love is the purpose
It's the purpose to plan blessing
The place of purpose
Hear me, there is love
And it's in my purpose
Love is my purpose

LOVE IS A DUKE

Love is a duke who comes to a house
A duke who is blessing
A duke who sees a house and blesses
A duke who blesses
A duke who blesses

Love is a duke who heeds my words
And love is he who loves a nation
Love is hearing and love is hearing
Love is a duke who commands blessing

LOVE IS A GREAT BUILDING

Love is a great building
Love is a building of love
Oh love rests in this place
Love is as the blessed ones
In this place

Love is as a house for me to be
Love is a work of grace
Love is a house
It's a house for words of grace

Love is a house of cast-offs
Love is a place for these now
Love is an operation in this place
Love is an operation
What an operation!

Love is bread, love is wine
Love is bread and great, great wine
For love, love, love is
A great feast, feast, feast

Love is a great feast you come to
Love is a feast: blessed, blessed, blessed
Love is a feast for you to be
Love is a feast
You are open to come in

IT'S A MATCH

It's a match
God says it's a match
Love is a match of least and these
It's a match of words and love

It's a match of not and yes
Love is a match
Of bread and the wine
It's a match of love and sharing
Daddy loves, daddy loves

It's a match of what and where
Love is a match of bread and grapes
Love is a match of growing
It's a match of blessing

Love is a shade
Match is a shade
It's a shade of love
It's a shade of love

LOVE SUP

Love sup, oh love sup!
It's a sup of words
It's a sup of grace
It's a sup of healing
But it's a sup of me

LOVE-APPLE

Love-apple
Love-apple is a word
I love the apple
The apple of my blessing

Love-apple: oh who is this?
They are these who are in me
Love-apple: oh they are me!
God says they are open to me

I am in they
And they are in my blessing
Love is the apple
Oh but love is great

Love is the who and love is the they
They who are, they who are
Love is the apple of my power
Love operates here for them

A CUP OF SOUP

A cup of soup, a cup of soup
It's in love, it's love that's in a soup
It's love that's in a soup
It's love that's in a soup you see

And it's love that's in your soup
It's love that's in the soup
It's love that's in the soup
It's love that's in the soup

It's love that's in the man
That has this soup
It's love that's in the soup
That's in the love

LOVE AND HONEY

Love is in a honey
And love is in my secret
Love is in a honey
And love is in my secret
Love is in the honey that you receive
Love is in the honey that you receive

Love is a word but it's as honey
It's as the honey, it's as the honey
It's as the honey, it's as the honey
It's as you receive, receive my honey
Receive my honey, receive my honey
Receive my honey, receive my honey
Receive my honey, receive my love

Love is as the honey you receive
And love you receive, receive is
Love, oh love is in the honey
And love is oh, oh yes!

It is mmm…mmm…yes
Oh, oh, oh yes
And love mmm…mmm, yes
Oh, mmm…yes, mmm
Oh mmm…eh…mmm!
Mmm! Seek love, seek love
Mmm! Seek love, seek love!

LOVE IS AS A SEED

Love is as a seed in the mill
Love is the seed in the mill
Love is turning, turning in the mill
Love is turning, blessing, blessing
Love is abiding in the mill
Love does grow as a seed
It's a seed that's the mill

It turns blessing
It turns blowing
It turns love
It turns into blessing
It turns into change
It turns into a purpose
It turns into a love-loaf
It turns into a loaf of blessing

LOVE BREAD

Love bread
It's words
It's grace
It's heart
Love bread is seed
Love bread is change
Love bread is commerce to nations
Love bread is most great
Love bread is more love
Oh love bread you're to receive

LOVE GUTS

Love guts, love guts
Love guts, love guts
I love guts—guts in this house
Guts in this place

I love your purpose
I love your blessings
I love your name
I love your nation

Love is the maker
Love is a meeting of this and that
Love is as a blade, a blade of grass
Love is as a leader
Who receives my purpose

Love is as a leader who worships
Love is a leader who prays
Love is as one who says
This is not the way

They say this is not the way
Layman, layman, layman
The layman is the one who is the one
Who is the one?

He is the one who goes
He is the one who goes
And goes and goes
He is the one in the nation

Love is me. Love is me, me, me!
Love is me, me, me!
Love is me
Oh you! Receive!!

Love is open and it is open
And it is open
And it opens a church
Money? Love is sending finance
Love is sending the finance

Love is demonstrating
Love is demonstrating great grace
Love is amber that is healing
Love is a word that is seeing

Love is a word
But it is my abundance
Love is abundance
It's an abundance of finances

Love…is it done?
But now it increases
They say love is in a generation
They say love is a bite
But it is me

They say love is a meeting
But it is me
Love is an abundance of visitations
Love says: it's guts

Love says: it's guts to do
It's guts to prophesy
it's guts to pray
Love is guts, love is guts

I will tell you
That love is guts

LOVE IS NUMB

Love is numb for it is love
It's in the man
It's in the man who is in me
He sees me, he sees me

He sees things for as I see
He sees things in me
He knows me, he knows them
He knows the nations

The nations, the nations
He knows all things
For he knows, he knows
He knows—oh how he knows

He knows love
Oh he knows what is
He sees ways, ways
He sees a great way

He sees what to do
He sees the labor of the church
He sees love come today
He sees love come

He sees the turn of the need
He sees the need, need, need
He sees the need
He says for now
I will turn my power

And now love will come in
And love will, love will, love will
Tumble, tumble this, tumble that
Tumble this and that

Love will tumble a change
Love tumbles, love tumbles
It tumbles, tumbles, tumbles
Love is tumbling: it's new and now

Love says now will I seed

LOVE IS AN ADDING

Love is an adding
Love is an add—what an add!
Love is an add of words
It's an add of words
Love is an add of words
And abundance
Love is an add in the generations
Love is an add…for you are in me

LOVE IS A BURDEN

Love is a burden
I'm in this
Burden for grace
Burden for operations
It's a burden for love
It's a burden for love
I'm bringing you love
Love is a burden

LOVE WORKING

Love is work, love is work
Love is work, love is work
It's work, yes, it's work

It's work of purpose
It's work of abundance
And it's work of abundance

It's work to turn a purpose
It's work to turn a house
It's work to turn a purpose
It's work to turn a house

Love is a command to do
It's to do
It's a command to do
And to do is to do

It's to have love in this
For it is the power in grace
And grace opens a house

And love answers a command
Love commands, love commands
And it commands a turn

Love is water, it flows in purpose
It flows a house, it flows a church
It flows your city, it flows a church

A church of love, a church of purpose
A church of love, a church of purpose
Love commands you in me

Love will turn, love will turn
Love is in me, love is in me
Love does turn me: it grows a church

Love you, love you, love you
Love you, love you
Yes, I open love up…today is the day

The old, the old who say it's this
It's a cut, it's a cut
They say it's not this
It's not this now

They say it's not now
I love, love is now
It's now for this day
It's now, it is now for this

They say gun, gun, gun, gun
I say love, love, love, love
They say it's cutting, it's cutting me

Oh it cuts me, it cuts me
Oh they say it cuts
I say I receive you

They say the door
It's the door you go
I say today, I say

Come I say come, I do receive
They say oh this is in that
I say I am in them

Love Working - (continued)

Love says come in, it says come in
And come and come to me
Unto me and me and me
Come in, come in, come in, come in

Today! Today! Today! Today!
Today! Today! Today! Today!
Today! Today is now!

It's now abiding today
It's now love increase
It's now blessing increase

I'm calling in my love
I'm calling love
I'm calling love to your house

Love here, love here
More and more love here
Loving, loving, double love
It's now double love

Double love for you
It's double my love
My love for you

LOVE IS A WORSHIP!!

Love is a worship
It is love when you worship
It is love when you prophesy
The winds are blustery
As you worship, I do for you
Your worship is love

LOVE IS BLUSTERY GRACE

Love is a time of blustery grace
Love is a time of wonder-change
Love is a time for me to see
And is a time for words to be

LOVE IS A DOUBLE-DEED

Watch, love is a double-deed
It's a word and it's a great word
Love is as a seed
Love is as a reed
Love is as up
Love is as work
Love is as a knit
Love is as a lead
Love is as a reed
Love is as new-love is as woo
Love is as dear and love is as where
God says love is as me
And love is as you!

LOVE IS A KEY

Love is a key that opens a door
Love is a key, you open to see
Love is a door that opens for you
Oh love is a key to open and see

Love is a key that opens you to me
Love is a key you send out
Love is a key you turn and turn
Love is a key you open to me

Love is a key you're to see and do
Love is a key to the nations
You open and open
Love is a key you open and turn

Love is a key
You're to love
Love is a key
You're to share the key

LOVE IS A LINE

Love is a line
Love is a line for the church
It's a line of lead
It's a line today

Love is a line that increases the nation
It's a line for your church to be
Love is a line for your nation to be
Love is a line the word says

Love is a line of words and grace
Love is a line to go and be
For love is a great line
And it's a line

Lay it! Lay it! Lay it! Lay it!
Lay the line, lay the line
Lay the line and lay it now
Lay the line and time comes now

Line you! Line you with me
And line you with my blessings
Receive, line you with me
And line with see

Line, line
Line, line
Line my son
Line you with me

LOVE FORCES A SITUATION

Love forces a house to me
Love is a force
It's a force of purpose
Love is a force
It's a force of blessing

LOVE IS AN OPERATION

Love is an operation
It's a broad thing
Love is an operation
Of leaders in grace
Love is an operation
Of hearts and words

But love is an operation
Of love-healings
Love is an operation
Of heat and grace
Love is an operation
Of healing leaps
Love is an operation
Leap! Leap!

Love is an operation
Of utter grace
Love is an operation
For these and thee
Love is an operation
Oh come more to me!
It's an operation
You're to come and be

Love is an operation
Raising and raising!
Love is an operation
Here. There
Led. Led
But love is an operation

You are an operation
You are open to
Love here
Love operate
Love there
Love operate

LOVE IS OPERATING

Love is operating
It's abundant
Love is abundant—but answers
Love is miracles of blessing

And love blows 'n blows abundance
The battle is abundant
And the battle is open
And the battle is increased

And the mantle is abundant
These are many mercies
These are many blessings
Oh…abundant grace

New love, new love
A new love I send
Love blesses
Oh love blesses

LOVE IS A BEAST

Love is a beast
It's a blessing
Love is a beast
But it's me
Love is a beast
Working in the nations

Love is a beast
Keeping man
Love is a beast
Keeping them
Love is a beast
Shedding and shedding

Love is a great, great beast!

LOVE IS A MANTLE

Love is a mantle
It's a mantle of power
It's a mantle of healing
It's a mantle of leaders
It's a mantle of abundance

Oh they say 'the mantle'
But it is my power
It's power-abundant
It's power to church
My power to change the house

They say who receives this?
For it is for these
But it is for they
They who see me
The mantle is for they

It's for they who are
For they who are my seed
For they who are my seed
They who are my seed—my word
They who are my word and my sons

Love is in them
And love is in these
These who are open to me
These who are open to be
These who are open to me

My! My! My time!
For this to be
This is the day for mantles
But it's for these in me
Abiders—they abide

They abide in my power
They abide in my blessing
They abide in abundance
And they open themselves to me
Mighty, mighty they are!

They are mighty to receive
They are mighty in abundance
And they are mighty with me!
They say where is the mantle?
Where is they?

They say where are they?
It is in them who are in me
Love is in the mantle
And they are with me
But they are in worship

And they are worshipping
My blessing, my church
The Master says they are
They are…me
They are…in me

They blend
They blend in the nations
Muttering blessings
They are in my grace
They are in my blending

And they are opening themselves
They open themselves to me
I send you love, I send you love
But you are to receive
Love hears these things

LOVE IS AN AID FOR AIDS

Love is an aid for things
Love is an aid in grace
Love is an aid for you
But love is an aid in this

Many, many things they are in
And many are the things they do
But I am love, but I am love
God says I love to love them

This is a door—grace!
Love is a great, great door
Love is a door for they
Love is a door for they to come

Love is a door for they to come
Master, Master
I am open
I am open to they

Yea! Yea! Love says yea!
Love says yea!
I am open to they
I am open to they with these things

Lads, lads, and lads
God is word, God is word
You're in an arid house
But I am open to you

You're not in this
You're not in this
You're open to be
You're open...receive

God says love opens this
Oh, oh I open this
I open these
I open these

I open these lads
I open these ladies
Yeah, I open these
Oh I open these to be

For they will know, for they'll know
For they will know and they will see
They will see I AM
They will see I AM

For I am blessing for they to see
They will see this grace
They will see my blessing
They will see my love

They will see abundance of grace
They'll see operations of abundance
They will see operations of healings
They will see operations of my love

They will know I love they
They will receive and receive
Love will turn this
Love will turn they

Love will heal they
Love is the love for this
Love is the grace for this
Love come, they will come

They will turn
It's the thing you receive
They say oh this!
God says they will receive

Soon they will see
They will see, they will see
They will know I AM
Oh they will receive

LOVE IS A SEED

Love is a seed, love is a seed
But it's a seed-working
Your word is the key to grace
Your words are the seeds to grace

But my seed is me
And the seed is in you
And love is a seed: oh my seed
It's a seed of rest and rest and rest

Love is a seed in this
It's a seed in thee
Love is a seed: it's me…it's you!
Love is a seed blessing in thee
Love seed—you are in me

It's a seed of grace and power
Love is a seed
But it's a great change
But love operates in you

Love opens as the seed
Oh love is as the seed in you
Oh watch me increase
Increase as this seed
Let it go up, let it go up

Let it open up
Let it open up
The seed operates
It operates as you change

Oh the seed opens
Increase and abundance
Oh love you are in me
Oh love you are open

Receive!

LOVE IS BRINGING

Love is bringing new change
Love is bringing things of worship
Love is bringing great abundance
And love hears in this

They say why they do this?
Why they do that?
I say I am in this
I command the blessing
I command great power
I command the visitation
I command the bring
I command the purpose
Yea, I command the purpose

Love will bring it
It's love that brings the finances
It's love that commands graces
It commands abundance

LOVE IS A SIGN AND WONDER

Love is a sign
And love is a wonder
It's a sign, it's a wonder
It's a sign, it's wonder

It's a sign, it's a wonder, it's me!
Love is a wonder, a wonder of grace
And love is a sign
A sign of the nation

JOY BRINGS

Joy brings, joy brings
Joy brings love
Joy brings dreams
Joy brings dreaming dreams

But blessing is blessed
Love is in blessing
And love is broad and broad
Love is blessing and blessing
And love is more and more

Love is meeting me
Love is meeting me
Love is broad and love is broad
Love is more and more

LOVE IS JOY

Love is joy
The joy for me
It's joy I have

Love is man in me
And love is man in joy
Love is—oh love is a joy!
Love is joy, oh what joy!
But love is joy and joy is great!

Love is open! Receive it!
Love is greater, it is greater
Love is a joy to receive!

LOVE IS AN AROMA

Love is an aroma
Oh what is this aroma?
It's the aroma of abundance
The aroma of abundant love
The aroma of great blessing
Love is a sum of great aromas
It's an abundance of words
Abundance and love
It's an immersing
What is it you see?
It's an aroma blessing you

LOVE IS A SCENT

Love is a scent
It's a scent of grace leading grace
Love is a scent
A great scent of great love

Love is a great scent
Love is a scent
Oh what a scent it is
Love is a scent

Oh smell the words
Smell the grace
Love is a word, but it is me
Love is a great operation of scents

Love is a scent
Of great showings of love

LOVE IS A PRINTING

Love is a printing
Oh what is it?
Love is a printing
Of my blessing

Love is in the print
Love is in the words
Love is in a rest in me
And love is in the words I send

And love is old, but it is me
And love is a word for the days
And love is a word for the days
And the days and the days

Love is a word for hours
Love is a word here and there
Love is a watch
It is a watch of my grace

Love is blessing who they are
Love is blessing
But it is love in the word
Love is my words to the nations
Love is my word to your church

Love is blessing these
Love is blessing where you are
Love is broad and love is broad!
Love is broad and it is abundant

Love is broad and it is love
Love is broad and broad is it!
Love is new and love is new
Love is a word for you

Love is a word for you and they
Love is a word that you say
Love is now and love is now
Love is a blot on the church

Love is a blot, a blot of blessing
Love is great, oh great!
Love is as you see my word
And love is as you receive my words

Love is blending a we and we
Love is blending this and that
And love is blending words and work
And love is blending a rose and a rose

For love is a blend of this and that
And love is a blending
Of my blessing and change
And love is a blending of me and you
For love is a blend

Oh what a blend!

LOVE IS SHAKING

Love is shaking
For love is power
For God is great
And God is changing

Oh love is sharing
Love is greater
And greater and greater
Love is changing

And love is working
And love is working
Leap in grace and leap for grace
It's a love-grace

Love is a great shaking
It's a great shaking
It's a great love
It's love-show…it's a great show

Night is shedding
For it's great today
Love is showing
For it's abundant

God is great
For he is great
It's great to love
Love is odd, for it is open

Love is balance
Love is balance
For love is blessing
And love is sharing

God is love and he is love
Blending, blending
Love is a great open grace
Love is a secret for the house

And love is a secret for your seed
Love is a love-sharing
For love is a showing
And love is showing, love is showing

Love blending: it's great for this
Love is a blend
It's a blend of healings
For love blends, shares and loves

Love hears and love operates
Blessed, blessed, blessed operation
Lady, lady, love these
Lady, lady, love me

Love leads, love leads
Love sets change
It's love in grace
Make it love: you're to make it love

LOVE IS WATER

Love is water: it's a flowing grace
Love is water that flows to you
And love is a flow of blessing
But love is a flow
Of abiding abundance

Waters flow with me doing
Waters flow with me being
Waters flow with blessings coming
Oh the flow of my abundance

Love is a flowing secret
Oh flowing in my blessings
The flow of healings
The flow of love

The flow of visitations
The flow of operations
Must God do? Must God flow?
Yes. Flow-worship; flow-abundance
The flow of my blessings open today

THE WATERS OF POWER

But the water is showing
The water is going and it's coming
It's the waters of power
It's the waters of love
It's love and it's love

God is showing
The MASH, the M.A.S.H.
It's the great healing power
The great healing power
Love is as the waters of power

LOVE IS WIPING

Love is wiping
Love is a wiping of things
Love is a wiping of this from that
Love is a great wiping of the sin
For love is the blessing to have

Love is the wipe for the nation
Love is the wipe for your church
Love is the wipe you have
Love is the wipe for the cussing
Love is the wipe for Britain

Love is the wipe for the rapper
Love is the wipe for the shady
Love is the wipe for Iran
For love is the wipe of nations
It's love for these, it's love for you

It's love for he
But it's love for she
Love is a great wipe
But it's water, it's words
But it's water, it's words

It's the blood, it's the blood
It's the blood, it's the blood
Oh the blood
It's words, it's words
But it's the blood

Love is a wipe
It wipes what reeks
It's a wipe of things
It's a wipe of things
Love wipes this—love wipes that

Oh wipe!
What they say?
What they say? Oh wipe
God wipes: he's a-wiping
I am sending wipings

MUTTER, MUTTER, MUTTER

They say mutter, mutter, mutter
They say what is this?
They say things about me
They say I am an old thing

They say old, I am old
Love is a word—a sending word
Love is a word of great power
Knitting, knitting, love is knitting

They say this is not me
They say God is not
They say done, done, God is not

But I, I-AM-THAT-I-AM
I AM abundant
I AM love
They say eliminate

They say eliminate
Eliminate this, eliminate that
They say eliminate this word
They say eliminate the word

But I say I-AM-THAT-I-AM
I AM blessing
I AM love, I AM love

Job, job, job, job
Oh they say, it's the job
But I, but I
But I AM in this visitation

They say it's this house
But I, but I, but I AM in this secret
They say job, job, job
They say it is the job

I say love, love, love
I say love this, love them
I say love them
And love for me

Oh they say it's the day
It's the day
Oh what day!
They say these days are

There's a no, there's a no
There's a no, there's no
They say no to me—no

Knock, I send a knock
I send a knock
I send a knock
They say but it's this

It's the generation
It's the generation
That comes: opening up
The maker is love

He sends them
He sends them
He sends them and he sends them

There's mercy for this nation
There's mercy for this nation
There's mercy for this nation
There's mercy for this nation

There's mercy for the house
There's mercy for the house
There's mercy for the house
There's mercy for the house

Yes, yes, yes, and yes
I send great mercy
But mercy opens up love
Mercy opens up love

VOICES

Blood! They say blood
And they say blood
But they're voices
And they are voices

The voice of the one
The voice of the one
Who is in this purpose
The voice of the nation

Saying oh now more
Come more
They say it's a joy to do
It's a joy to be

They say love is a door for the nation
They say oh I am open to this
They say love is an open love
They say oh I am open to this

Love is a king who sees
Love is a word—heed!
Love is a here and now
Love is a vast grace

Love is a meeting where I am

LOVE POETRY FROM GOD

Love is a change
To love is to receive
Love is a word, for it is purpose
Love is a blessing
There is love in blessing

I am abiding now, you see
Love is the key to my blessing
You are loved and you are loved
Love is a word they say
But love is the key to my grace, I say

Love is blessed, it's a great thing
It's a great thing to bless
The church is now a love house
There's love to receive
Love to dream

Love blows in
And it blows into a church
Love will command grace
God is love, he is love
Greater has come

Oh yes, oh yes, greater has come
Love is now
There is a love in the nation
That will come
It's love days, it's love days

Love grows the church
Love grows the house
It's love that grows here
Love on you, love on you
I do, I do, love on you

Love is an answer, it is the answer
It's love, it's doing, it does, it goes
It goes into houses
It goes into a house
It works and it works

Love Poetry From God - (continued)

Love is a command
It does for it is
Love commands you to receive
Love commands things to open
Love commands dreams and dreams

I love the apple, for you are
I love to dream things
For this you are
I love in my abundance
And love hands things

Greater and greater is the power
For it is love
They labor for they say
It's this, it's that
I say love, blessing, increasing

It increases the church
Love will command them to come
It increases a house
Love opens a church
It opens leaders

It opens power
It raises churches
Love is fire, fire, fire
It changes a past
They say it's guns

I say it's love
It's a need
It's a need
But love is a seed
They say cut them

But I say love
Increase
You're ready to receive
You're ready for me
Loving them is a key

Blessing now
Receive
They say love is lips
But I say it's power
And change

I love things in you
I love you for you
You are in me, you are in my grace
Love does for you, it does in you
Love answers it

I'm in love in this
I'm in love in this
I love ones who purpose to preach
Love is the key to the heart
Love you, love you, I love to do

Love is a turn: it turns things
It will increase
The blessed shut me
They say not this
Love says yes. Love says yes

Love commands, yes!
It commands to change
Oh command!
It commands to change
Love says God is...He is

NOW IT'S A DAY OF LOVE

Love is a thing
Now it's a day
And what a day it is
A day of work
A day of work in my purpose
A day of work in my blessing

Love is in the air
For it's in the word
There is a loving love
This is a love of love

It's greater than what you see
It's greater than what you turn to
It's greater than what you know

WHAT TIME IS IT?

They say it's now late
But it's now love time
It's me time! It's now time!
It's God time!

They say it is not time
They say not now
But I say it's my time
It's my time! It's my time!
It's my time!
It's my time!

It's great time
It's me time
It's my time
It's me time
It's love time

Love is a time…
But it's my time…

THE HOUR IS NOW

The hour is now
They say it's in this time, that time
Love says now
Where, where, they say
But I say it's in this, it's in them
They say it is in that and it's in that
But I say it is in them, those who say
It is in this, I say it is in them

Love is in them
They are to see love is in them
As they see, as they see
Love, purpose; love, power
As they see, as they see
Love, purpose; love, power
Love abides, it abides
It abides, for they see

And they see, and they see
And they see that it's me

They see and they do
They do and do
For as they do they see
They know it's me that is in them
Who they are, is me
It's me in them, they see it's me
For they stir themselves to see
They stir themselves to see and be

Now is day, it is day to do
To do, to do
To do my word
In power and grace
To do my word
In power and grace
Now the day, it's now the day
Now the day, it's now this day

WORDS OF LOVE

LOVE IS NOT LATE

They say love is late
But I am now!
I am in this
I am in this
I am in this

Yeah, I am in that
Oh they say that it is now late
But love says now I am
Love will turn your house to be
Love will turn your house to me

Double love!
Double love!
It's coming to you!
Double love! Double love
It's coming to you!

Love…
That great abundance
Which opens and heals!

LOVE IS A TIME

Love is a time for you to see
And love is a time to do and see
It's a time to do, it's a time to do
A time of abundance

A time to be
I say to be
Oh love, oh love
Oh love, oh love!

IT'S LOVE TODAY

Today is love
It's today a visit
It's a visit of blessing
It's today love is great
It's today love is great
Sending love
I'm sending love
Hear my son, hear my words
Love is a blessing
This is love: that I-AM
I am love, I am love
I am love and I love
I love your seed
They have the blessing
They are the door; their doors open
Their doors open and they receive
They are come to my blessing
They are loved in my blessing
This is love
Love is man in my blessing
Love increases in the house
Love turns a blessing
Love opens you
Love leads in blessing
Love leads you
To bring my grace to them
There's love here, there's love there
Say that love is in this day
It's love to receive

LOVE TIMES LOVE

Love times love is love
Love times love is love
Love is great for as you say it
It answers things
It answers a place
Oh it answers a church
Oh it answers a house

Love is a heart
It's a heart of power
Love is a place for me to do
Love is a place of abiding power
Love is a word of purpose today
Love is a word of great abiding
Love is a heart that is in me
It's a word…but
it's me

RAIN, RAIN, RAIN

Rain, rain, rain, rain
Rain, rain, rain, rain
It's a rain of love
It's a rain of love

A love that comes
A love that comes
It's a love that blesses
A love will come on the nations

A love of abundance
A love of greater change
It's a love that turns a church to me
It's a love that turns a church to be

Love is rain, love is rain
Love is rain in the church
Love is rain in the church
Oh! It rains in the church

Oh! It rains in the church
Oh what rain! It comes in love
It rains now, it's the rain that you see
It's rain, but it is purpose

Oh! What is the rain they say?
It's me, me, me, me!
It's rain doing
It's me being, it's me abiding

Love is the rain
That you know you see
Arid, arid, but now it's time
It's now time for me
Love is in the rain, love is in the rain

Oh! Words, words, words now
Words, words, words, words
Words, words, words, words
Words of purpose

Words of grace
Words of blessing
And words of blessing
It's words of abundance

There's words of lead
But there's words of purpose
Soak in blessing
Soak in abundance

And love is in this rain
And love is in this rain
Yes, love is in the rain
God is love and love is in the rain

Oh what is this love?
Love is the power
Love is the power to turn a house
It's the power to turn a church

Love is an hour now is
And love is a power now come
A God who does, a God who is
Row, row, row, in this

Row in the word, row in me
Hear my words and row in me
Love is a word: it's as you row
Love is a word: it's as you row
Blessings increase and come this day

Rain, Rain, Rain - (continued)

As you love
It comes to you
It comes, it comes
As the words of rain

Love is in the words of rain
Love is in the words of rain
Love, yea! Love, yea!
Love yea! Love yea!

Love yea! Love yea!
Love, it's now the rain
Love is in the purpose of the rain
Love is the rain

Love is in this rain
Love is in now time
Love is in my time
Love is in me—for you are...see!

Love, love
Ah-ha! Ah-ha!
It's love now
Love...ah-ha!

THE MAN

Love is abundant
But it's in me
Love is a blessing...oh it's to receive
Love is a blowing in
It's time to know
Love is a change you are seeing

They say the man
I say son, the man is blessed
He is me
He is me
They say the man is open
The man is in

The man is in
The man is in
He says, he says
But they say bought, bought, bought
They say he's a sell-out
But I say he is in me

They say he's in this and that
I say he is the purpose
He is the one
They say will he, will he?
I say he is a purpose
He is a great one

God says
"The man, the man is the one"

MARCHING, MARCHING, MARCHING

Saddle and saddle
And go and go
Go and go
Open and go
Go and go into houses and houses

Go and go into nations and nations
Go and go into churches and nations
Go and do
Go and be

Share your thoughts

Feel free to judge this work by way of the Holy Scriptures and prayer. And if you would like to share how this collection of poetry has blessed you, as well as any prayer requests you may have, please write to me at:

PO Box 441648
Indianapolis, Indiana 46244
United States of America

theseer1959.wordpress.com

twitter.com/theseer1959

www.ingramcontent.com/pod-product-compliance
Lightning Source LLC
Chambersburg PA
CBHW081346040426

42450CB00015B/3323